ORDAINING WOMEN.

By Rev. B.T. ROBERTS, A.M.

Editor of "THE EARNEST CHRISTIAN,"
Author of FISHERS OF MEN,
WHY ANOTHER SECT, ETC.

"There is neither Jew nor Greek,
there is neither bond nor free,
there is neither male nor female:
for ye are all one in Christ Jesus."
- Galatians iii, 28.

Original printing 1891, Rochester, NY
EARNEST CHRISTIAN PUBLISHING HOUSE.

ISBN 0-89367-176-2

Reproduction 1992
Second printing 2003
Light and Life Communications
Indianapolis, IN 46253-5002

TO

MY BELOVED WIFE,

WHO FOR FORTY-TWO YEARS

HAS FAITHFULLY STOOD BY ME IN THE GOSPEL MINISTRY,

Who has never shunned to be a partaker of the

AFFLICTIONS OF THE GOSPEL,

But has faced undismayed the fires of persecution,

WHO HAS BEEN TO ME A CONSTANT INSPIRATION

TO A FULLER UNDERSTANDING OF THE

Mysteries of the Kingdom,

THESE PAGES ARE AFFECTIONATELY DEDICATED

BY THE AUTHOR.

CONTENTS.

FOREWORD

In hindsight, *Ordaining Women* was B.T. Roberts'
most prophetic book. He was wrestling in 1891 with
issues that still stir the church. He gives clear biblical
answers to opponents of total equality for women in
all functions of church leadership and authority.

Roberts' advocacy of unfettered women's ministry began early in his ministry. In an 1872 pamphlet,
The Right of Women to Preach the Gospel, Roberts bibli-
cally supported full equality for women in the life of
the church. "One cause of [the] comparative ineffi-
ciency of the Gospel," he argued, "is found in the
proscription of woman — a relic of barbarism — to
which enlightened, Christian people still tenaciously
cling." Roberts maintained that "The Gospel gives to
woman the same religious rights that it does to man.
It allows of no distinction on account of sex or social
condition." Thus the "claim of a woman to be called
of God to preach the Gospel should not ... be re-
jected because she is a woman. Apply to her the
same tests that you apply to man." The relevant is-
sue is not gender, but rather calling and gifts.

Here Roberts was a minority voice in both the
Methodist Episcopal and the Free Methodist denominations. Yet, Benson Roberts notes, *The Right of
Women to Preach the Gospel* "had a wide circulation,
was widely quoted and helped to break down the
barriers of prejudice." Women especially were encouraged: "Many who faltered and hesitated to face
the inevitable opposition have been strengthened to
obey the heavenly calling" (Benson Roberts, *Benjamin
Titus Roberts,* 530).

B.T. Roberts also celebrated the lives of women
preachers whom he saw as models. When Mrs. Jane
Shuart Dunning of New York's Providence Mission
died, Roberts wrote that she was "one of the first,

ablest and most useful preachers" of early Free Methodism, having planted churches in Binghamton, NY, and Dover, NJ, before beginning ministry among New York's urban poor. Through her ministry many "were converted, and many were sanctified to God" (*The Earnest Christian*, Feb. 1891, 37-41).

Roberts narrowly lost the debate over women's ordination at the 1890 Free Methodist General Conference. Thus, though frail in health, he published *Ordaining Women* in 1891. Roberts "was in advance of his own church," Benson noted. Not until the General Conference of 1974 did the Free Methodist Church come to agree with its founder, finally granting full equality to women by simply deleting the restrictive wording from the *Discipline*.

Howard A. Snyder

Professor of History and Theology of Mission,
Asbury Theological Seminary, KY;
Chair of the Committee on Free Methodist History and Archives;
Author, *Populist Saints: B.T. and Ellen Roberts and the First Free Methodists*

PREFACE.

I have written this book from a strong conviction of duty. Christ commands us to let our light shine.

There is no reason why this subject should not be considered as calmly and candidly as any other. We should not refuse to examine it in the light of Scripture and of reason because of any apprehension of dreadful consequences if some women should be ordained. By the Friends, for over two hundred years, woman has been accorded the same rights as man, and yet she has lost none of her womanliness in consequence. Among no class of people are women more true, and modest, and domestic, and noble, and refined, and given to every good work than among them. Nowhere else can be found more beautiful, happy homes than in the Society of The Friends.

Nor need we have any fearful forebodings, if giving to women equal rights in the church should lead to giving her equal rights in the state. This experiment too has been tried.

United States senator Carey is reported as saying: "In the State of Wyoming woman has had the ballot for twenty years. None of the objections which are made to this extension of the suffrage had been found in actual practice, in his State, to have a good basis. The result there has been more than satisfactory. It was not true that women in general took no interest in the question of suffrage. Those who were not originally advocates of it exercise their privileges when they once received them. There was fully as large a proportion of women who voted in his State today as of men. Anything that related at all to their interests was sure to bring out the full vote. He thought that the women gave more thought to the subject than the men, and were more conscientious in the exercise of their right. Their influence was exercised always on the side of good government and for the selection of the best men for office. Their influence in politics was of such a character as to make men more circumspect in the transaction of the duties of public office. He added that it was a particularly good element in all municipal elections. Women, as a class, can never be on the side of corruption, of the ignorant and the criminal elements which have such control in the municipal affairs of the leading cities of the United States."[1]

I have purposely avoided all appeals to sentiment and to "the spirit of the age," and based my arguments mainly on the Word of God. Where texts have been interpreted contrary to the generally received meaning, reasons have been given, which, I trust, will be found satisfactory. I have endeavored to make everything plain.

I ask as a special favor of those who have decided not to agree with the position I have taken that they will read before they condemn. The subject is worthy of patient and prayerful investigation.

I have no misgivings as to the truth of what I have written, nor evil forebodings of the consequences that will result if the views herein advocated come to be generally received.

I only ask that truth may prevail, Christ be glorified, and His Kingdom be advanced on earth.

CHAPTER I.

PREJUDICE.

"Errors, like straws, upon the surface flow;
He who would search for pearls must dive below."

–Dryden.

"He that would seriously set upon the search of truth, ought in the first place to prepare his mind with a love of it, for he that loves it not will not take much pains to get it, nor be much concerned when he misses it."

–Locke.

CHRIST lays great stress upon the truth. It has in it a saving quality. *"Sanctify them through thy truth."*– John 17:17. It is not possible for us to be sanctified only as far as we open our hearts to receive the truth, and inwardly resolve to obey it. The Holy Spirit is the spirit of truth. Jno. 14:17.

"Let us," says the Duke of Argyl, "educate ourselves up to that high standard in the love of truth, under which we hate and disdain an intellectual fallacy as much as we hate and disdain a common lie."

Then, to the rights of women under the Gospel, as an important question, we should give our candid attention. If prejudiced, we should, as Daniel Webster said, "Conquer our prejudices." The feeling against woman's being accorded equal rights with man, is old and deeply rooted. Generally, among mankind, the law of force has been the prevailing law. The stronger have tyrannized over the weaker.

Aristotle was one of the greatest of the old Greek philosophers. In his book on Politics and Economics he wrote: "By nature some beings command, and others obey, for the sake of mutual safety; for a being endowed with discernment and forethought is, by nature, the superior and governor; whereas he who is merely able to execute by bodily labor is the inferior and a *natural slave;* and hence the *interest of master and slave is identical.*"[2]

"It is clear then, that some men *are free by nature, and others are slaves, and that in the case of the latter, the lot of slavery is both advantageous and just.*"[3]

Again, Aristotle wrote: "The art of war is, in some sense, a part of the art of acquisition; for hunting is a part of it, which it is necessary for us to employ against wild beasts, and *against those of mankind who, being intended by nature for slavery, are unwilling to submit to it, and on this occasion, such a war is by nature just.*"[4]

Until recently, as long as there was any slavery to tolerate, human slavery was tolerated by the leading churches of this country. Reason and revelation were appealed to in defence of the practice of human slavery. No longer ago than 1836 the General Conference of the M. E. Church took the following action, as recorded on its journal:

"Resolved by the delegates of the Annual Conferences in General Conference assembled:

1. That they disapprove, in the most unqualified sense, the conduct of two members of the General Conference who are reported to have lectured in this city recently upon, and in favor of modern Abolitionism.

2. That they are decidedly opposed to modern Abolitionism, and wholly disclaim any right, wish, or intention to interfere in the civil and political relation between master and slave as it exists in the slave holding States of this Union."

Some time after slavery was abolished by war, the above resolutions were repealed, and another General Conference of the same Church passed a resolution to the effect that it was a matter of congratulation that the Methodist Episcopal Church had always taken the lead of the sister churches in the anti-slavery movement.

About thirty years ago the Right Rev. John Henry Hopkins, D. D., LL. D., one of the learned men of his day, and the Protestant Episcopal Bishop of the diocese of Vermont, wrote and published a book in which he endeavored to prove that human slavery, as it then existed in these United States, was supported by "the authority of the Bible, the writings of the Fathers, the decrees of Councils, the concurrent judgment of Protestant divines, and the Constitution." The efforts to overthrow it he characterized as the "assaults of mistaken philanthropy, in union with infidelity, fanaticism, and political expediency."

If those who stood high as interpreters of Reason and Revelation, and who expressed the prevailing sentiment of their day, were so greatly mistaken on a subject which we now think so plain that it does not admit of dispute, that every man has a right to freedom, is it not possible that the current sentiment as to the position which WOMAN should be permitted to occupy in the *Church of Christ* may also be wrong?

Reader, will you admit this possibility? Will you sit as an impartial juror in the case, and carefully weigh the evidence we may present?

It has taken the world a long while to understand the Gospel of Jesus Christ; and even now it is but imperfectly understood.

We cannot ascertain the truth of an opinion by inquiries about its age. Let us decide that as the Church did, for ages, misinterpret the teachings of the Bible on the subject of slavery, so it may now fail to apprehend its teaching on the question of woman's rights.

Christian men and women should not wait until a righteous cause is popular before they give it their influence. Those who do, are simply following fashion, while they may think they are following the Lord.

"These loud ancestral boasts of yours,
How can they else than vex us?
Where were your dinner orators
When slavery grasped at Texas?
Dumb on his knees was every one
That now is bold as Caesar;
Mere pegs to hang an office on,
Such stalwart men as these are."

- Lowell.

It is not enough to say that the right will ultimately triumph; if we claim to be righteous we should help make the right triumph.

CHAPTER II.

WOMAN'S LEGAL CONDITION.

"There is who hopes (his neighbor's worth depressed),
Pre-eminence himself; and covets hence,
For his own greatness that another fall."

–Dante.

IN most nations, except Jewish and Christian, the condition of woman has been, from time immemorial, one of slavery. She was sold in marriage. Rome has given laws to the world, yet the young Roman, says Gibbon, "according to the custom of antiquity bought his bride of her parents, and she fulfilled the *co-emption* by purchasing, with three pieces of copper, a just introduction to his house and household deities." Her servitude was decorated by the title of "adoption," and, by a legal fiction, she became the "daughter" of her husband and the "sister" of her own children. Parental power in its fullest extent belonged to the husband in relation to the wife, as well as to the children. "By his judgment or caprice her behavior was approved or censured, or chastised; he exercised the jurisdiction of life and death; and it was allowed, that in the case of adultery or drunkenness, the sentence might be properly inflicted. She acquired and inherited for the sole profit of her lord; and so clearly was woman defined, not as a *person*, but as a *thing*, that, if the original title were deficient, she might be claimed, like other movables, by the *use* and possession of an entire year."[5]

The Spartan women were given the same physical training as men, and, as a consequence, they were more free in fact than the women of any other country of that age. "There can be little doubt," says Mill, "that Spartan experience suggested to Plato, among many other of his doctrines, that of the social and political equality of the sexes." Still, by law, in Sparta, as in the rest of Greece, the state of woman was that of subjection.

Stanley, writing of Central Africa, says: "Though a woman is as much a chattel in these lands as any article their lords may own, and is priced at from one to five head of cattle, she is held in honor and esteem, and she possesses rights which may not be overlooked with impunity. The dower stock may have been surrendered to the father, but if she be ill used she can easily contrive at some time to return to her parents, and before she be restored, the husband must repurchase her, and as cattle are valuable, he is likely to bridle his temper. Besides, there is the discomfort of the cold hearth, and the chilly arrangement of the household, which soon serve to subdue the tyrant."[6]

Though Christianity has greatly ameliorated the condition of woman, it has not secured for her, even in the most enlightened nations, that equality which the Gospel inculcates. A writer of only thirty years ago said: "The German women of the lower, and to some extent of the middle classes, are subjected to greater hardships than the women of any other nation of Europe. The farm laborer, the mechanic, and even the small farmer, makes his wife or mother his drudge, and compels her to perform the most menial and severe labors, while he sits or walks by her side unemployed, smoking his pipe. Within a few years, American citizens have witnessed, in Vienna, women acting as masons' tenders, carrying bricks and mortar up to the walls of lofty brick buildings in course of erection."[7]

John Stuart Mill, an English writer of highest authority, says:

"By the old laws of England, the husband was

called the lord of the wife; he was literally regarded as her sovereign, inasmuch that the murder of a man by his wife was called treason (petty as distinguished from high treason), and was more cruelly avenged than was usually the case with high treason, for the penalty was burning to death. Because these various enormities have fallen into disuse (for most of them were never formally abolished, or not until they had long ceased to be practiced); men suppose that all is now as it should be in regard to the marriage contract; and we are continually told that civilization and Christianity have restored to the woman her just rights. Meanwhile the wife is the actual bondservant of her husband; no less so, as far as legal obligation goes, than slaves commonly so called. She vows a life-long obedience to him at the altar, and is held to it all through her life by law. Casuists may say that the obligation of obedience stops short of participation in crime, but it certainly extends to everything else. She can do no act whatever but by his permission, at least tacit. She can acquire no property but for him; the instant it becomes hers, even if by inheritance, it becomes *ipso facto* his. In this respect the wife's position under the common law of England is worse than that of slaves in the laws of many countries; by the Roman law, for example, a slave might have his *peculium*, which, to a certain extent, the law guaranteed to him for his exclusive use. The higher classes in this country give an analogous advantage to their women, through special contracts setting aside the law, by conditions of pin-money, etc., etc.; since parental feeling being stronger with fathers than the class feeling of their own sex, a father generally prefers his own daughter to a son-in-law who is a stranger to him. By means of settlements, the rich usually contrive to withdraw the whole or part of the inherited property of the wife from the absolute control of the husband; but they do not succeed in keeping it under her own control; the utmost they can do only prevents the husband from squandering it, at the same time debarring the rightful owner from its use. The property itself is out of the reach of both; and as to the income derived from it, the form of settlement most favorable to the wife (that called "to her separate use") only precludes the husband from receiving it instead of her; it must pass through her hands, but if he takes it from her by personal violence as soon as she receives it, he can neither be punished, nor compelled to restitution. This is the amount of the protection which, under the laws of this country, the most powerful nobleman can give to his own daughter as respects her husband. In the immense majority of cases there is no settlement, and the absorption of all rights, all property, as well as all freedom of action, is complete. The two are called "one person in law," for the purpose of inferring that whatever is hers is his, but the parallel inference is never drawn that whatever is his is hers; the maxim is not applied against the man, except to make him responsible to third parties for her acts, as a master is for the acts of his slaves, or of his cattle. I am far from pretending that wives are in general no better treated than slaves; but no slave is a slave to the same lengths, and in so full a sense of the word, as a wife is. Hardly any slave, except one immediately attached to the master's person, is a slave at all hours and all minutes; in general he has, like a soldier, his fixed task, and when it is done, or when he is off duty, he disposes, within certain limits, of his time, and has a family life into which the master rarely intrudes. 'Uncle Tom' under his first master had his own life in his 'cabin,' almost as much as any man whose work takes him away from home, is able to have in his own family. But it cannot be so with the wife.

"What is her position in regard to the children in whom she and her master have a joint interest? They are by law his children. He alone has any legal rights over them. Not one act can she do towards or in relation to them, except by delegation from him. Even after he is dead she is not their legal guardian, unless he by will has made her so. He could even send them away from her, and deprive her of the means of seeing or corresponding with them, until his power was in some degree restricted by Sergeant Talfourd's act.

"This is her legal state. And from this state she has no means of withdrawing herself. If she leaves her husband, she can take nothing with her, neither her children nor anything which is rightfully her own. If he chooses, he can compel her to return by law, or by physical force; or he may content himself with seizing for his own use anything which she may earn, or which may be given to her by her relations. It is only legal separation by a decree of a court of justice, which entitles her to live apart, without being forced back into the custody of an exasperated jailer or which empowers her to apply any earnings to her own use, without fear that a man whom perhaps she has not seen for twenty years will pounce upon her some day and carry all off. This legal separation, until lately, the courts of justice would only give at an expense which made it inaccessible to any one out of the higher ranks. Even now it is only given in cases of desertion, or of the extreme of cruelty; and yet complaints are made every day that it is granted too easily."

It is no wonder that our prejudices against the rights of woman, coming down to us from such sources, and infused into us from early childhood, should be so strong. But reason and grace serve to overcome prejudice.

In no other nation of the world is woman's legal condition as favorable as in this country, yet in thirty-six of our states the woman with a husband living is not the legal owner of her children. The husband has the legal control, and in some of the states he can will the child away from his wife before the child is born.

CHAPTER III.

WORDS.

"I am not so lost in lexicography as to forget that words are the daughters of earth, and that things are the sons of Heaven."

– *Samuel Johnson.*

"*WORDS,*" says Bishop Berkeley, "have ruined and overrun all the sciences.

"To view the deformity of error we need only undress it," that is, deprive it of its verbal disguises.

"Howbeit that was not first which is spiritual, but that which is natural; and afterward that which is spiritual." – 1 Cor. 15:46.

This is true, not only of things, but of words which represent things. Πνεῦμα, *pneuma,* spirit, in its primary meaning signifies *wind, air, the air we breathe.*

Κῆρυξ, *kerux,* preacher, was a *herald,* who summoned the assembly and preserved order in it.

Ἀπόστολος, *apostolos,* apostle, was *one sent,* a messenger, envoy, ambassador.

Πρέσβυς, *presbus,* Πρεσβύτερος, *presbuteros,* elder, older, in the comparative degree, was one older than the most – one of mature years.

Ἐπίσκοπος, *episkopos,* bishop, was an overseer, watcher, guardian.

Διάκονος, *diakonos,* deacon, a servant, waiting-man or woman. The word is of common gender.

So we might go through with all the ecclesiastical terms of the New Testament. They all had, primarily, a secular meaning. But when it is evident that a writer gives to a word a special, secondary meaning, we must not in his writings, take that word in any place in its primary meaning, *unless the connection absolutely requires that we should.* To do so, in order to support a theory, is highly improper. It can never be done in the interests of truth.

To make a word mean one thing in one passage, and then something else in essentially the same connection, for the purpose of making the writer support our views, violates the principles of right interpretation. Locke says: "In all discourses wherein one man pretends to instruct or convince another, he should use the same word constantly in the same sense. If this were done (which nobody can refuse without disingenuity), many of the controversies in dispute would be at an end."[8]

But where it is clear that a word is used in its primary signification we should so understand it. Thus the word ἐκκλεσία, *ecclesia, church,* primarily, *assembly,* is found in the New Testament 115 times. It is properly translated church in all places except in Acts 19:32, 39, 41, where it evidently has its original meaning of Assembly.

"Fidelity in names," says Tertullian, "secures the safe appreciation of properties."

Words are arbitrary signs of ideas or of things. And often the same word represents things which have no relation to each other. The mother who brings up her children to obey her is sometimes obliged to use the *switch* upon the refractory child. The railroad man, by turning the *switch* wrong, wrecked the train. The fashionable woman when she buys a *switch* is careful to have it match her own hair.

The farmer cuts his wheat with a *cradle.* His wife rocks the baby in a *cradle.*

These illustrations show that in ascertaining the meaning of a word we must look at the connection in which it stands.

In our quotations we shall endeavor to give to words the signification intended by those who used them.

Unless we give to words their true meaning we cannot arrive at the truth for which we search. "I shall urge upon you," says Archbishop Trench, "how well it will repay you to study the words which you are in the habit of using or of meeting, be they such as relate to highest spiritual things, or the common words of the shop and the market, and of all the familiar intercourse of life. It will indeed repay you far better than you can easily believe."

"The study of words," says Max Muller, "may be tedious to the school-boy, as breaking of stones is to the wayside laborer: but to the thoughtful eye of the geologist these stones are full of interest; he sees miracles on the high road and reads chronicles in every ditch. Language, too, has marvels of her own, which she unveils to the inquiring glance of the patient student. There are chronicles below her surface; there are sermons in every word."

CHAPTER IV.

ORDINATION.

"No blood, no altar now,
  The sacrifice is o'er;
No flame, no smoke ascends on high,
  The Lamb is slain no more!
But richer blood has flowed from nobler veins,
To purge the soul from guilt, and cleanse the reddest stains."

—Bonar.

"Let all things be done decently, and in order."

—St. Paul.

DIFFERENT denominations hold different views about ordination.

1. The Friends have no sacraments and no ordained preachers. Their great theologian, Robert Barclay, says:

"When they assemble together, to wait upon God, and to worship and adore him; then such as the Spirit sets apart for the ministry, by its divine power and influence opening their mouths, and giving them to exhort, reprove and instruct with virtue and power: these are thus ordained of God and admitted into the ministry, and their brethren cannot but hear them, receive them, and also honor them for their work's sake."

He states as follows their position in reference to Baptism and the Lord's Supper:

"As there is one Lord and one faith, so there is one baptism; which is not the putting away the filth of the flesh, but the answer of a good conscience before God, by the resurrection of Jesus Christ. And this baptism is a pure and spiritual thing – to wit: the baptism of the Spirit and fire, by which we are buried with him, that being washed and purged from our sins, we may walk in newness of life; of which the baptism of John was a figure, which was commanded for a time, and not to continue forever."[9]

21

He takes a similar position in respect to the Lord's Supper:

"The communion of the body and blood of Christ is inward and spiritual, which is the participation of his flesh and blood, by which the inward man is daily nourished in the hearts of those in whom Christ dwells. Of which things the breaking of bread by Christ with his disciples was a figure, which even they who had received the substance used in the church for a time, for the sake of the weak; even as abstaining from things strangled, and from blood, the washing one another's feet, and the anointing of the sick with oil: all which are commanded with no less authority and solemnity than the former; yet seeing they are but shadows of better things, they cease in such as have obtained the substance."[10]

The main objection to this teaching is that it is contrary to the plain teaching of the New Testament. (1.) All true ministers are called of the Holy Ghost. But before one becomes a minister of the Gospel in the fullest sense, his divine call must be acknowledged and duly ratified by the church. Thus, the successor to Judas was so appointed, as described in Acts 1:15-26. Thus Paul was divinely called and in a formal manner publicly ordained. Acts 26:16-18 and Acts 13:2, 3.

(2.) *All* baptism *with* water is not John's baptism, as Robert Barclay teaches. Christian baptism is baptism *with* water. This is made perfectly clear. Paul, finding certain disciples at Ephesus, said unto them;

"Have ye received the Holy Ghost since ye believed? And they said unto him, We have not so much as heard whether there be any Holy Ghost.

"And he said unto them, Unto what, then, were ye baptized? And they said, Unto John's baptism.

"Then said Paul: John verily baptized with the baptism of repentance saying unto the people, that they should believe on him which should come after him, that is on Christ Jesus.

"When they heard this, they were baptized in the name of the Lord Jesus.

"And when Paul had laid his hands upon them, the Holy Ghost came on them; and they spake with tongues and prophesied"–Acts 19: 2-6.

Here three acts, each distinct in itself, are specified:

1. The baptism of John.
2. Baptism in the name of the Lord Jesus – that is Christian baptism.
3. The coming upon them of the Holy Ghost in His miraculous power.

This shows that the baptism of the Holy Ghost did not do away with baptism by water.

The same is also taught with equal plainness in Acts 10:47. "Can any man forbid water, that these should not be baptized which have received the Holy Ghost as well as we?"

Here were people who had received the substance; they needs must now receive the sign. They had been accepted in the army of the Lord; they must now publicly come under his banner.

They belonged to Christ; they must now, before their fellow men, receive the mark of Christ upon them.

(3.) Equally unscriptural is the above position in regard to the Lord's Supper. In it the body of Christ must be partaken of in a spiritual manner. But there must also be the outward sign.

"For I have received of the Lord that which also I delivered unto you, That the Lord Jesus the same night in which he was betrayed took bread: And when he had given thanks, He broke it, and said, Take, eat: this is my body which is broken for you; this do in remembrance of me. For as oft as ye eat this bread, and drink this cup, ye do show the Lord's death till he come. – 1 Cor. 11:23-26.

(1.) It was not figurative, but *actual bread which they ate. As oft as ye eat* – not *this*, indefinitely – but THIS BREAD.

(2.) They were to do this openly – not as a sacrifice for sin – but as a *remembrance of Christ*.

(3.) It was not to be "used in the church for a time, for the sake of the weak," but for ALL TIME – as long

23

as the world stands; for in doing this, *ye do shew the Lord's death till he come.*

As to "abstaining from things strangled and from blood, all Christians abstain from them; they still *wash one another's feet,* in the sense intended by our Lord; and some still anoint the sick with oil.

Many more passages to the same effect as the above might be quoted; but these are sufficient to show that the position taken by the Friends on the ministry and on the sacraments is contrary to the Scriptures.

2. THE ROMAN CATHOLICS. In striking contrast with the above views, is the teaching of the Church of Rome.

The Council of Trent, in the third canon of the twenty-third session, says:

"Whoever shall affirm that orders, or holy ordination are not a sacrament instituted by Christ the Lord, let him be accursed."

Again, in the fourth canon of the same session;

"Whoever shall affirm that the Holy Spirit is not given by ordination, let him be accursed."

As to the power conferred by ordination the Roman Catechism says:

"The faithful then are to be made acquainted with the exalted dignity and excellence of this sacrament in its highest degree, which is the priesthood. Priests and bishops are, as it were, the interpreters and heralds of God, commissioned in his name to teach mankind the law of God, and the precepts of a Christian life. They are the representatives of God upon earth. Impossible therefore, to conceive a more exalted dignity, or functions more sacred. Justly, therefore, are they called not only 'angels' but gods, holding as they do the place and power, and authority of God on earth. But the priesthood, at all times an elevated office, transcends in the new law all others in dignity. The power of consecrating and offering the body and blood of our Lord, and of remitting sins, with which the priesthood of the new law is invested, is such as cannot be comprehended by the human mind, still less is it equalled by, or assimilated to, anything on earth."[11]

"In ordaining a priest, the bishop, and after him, the priests who are present, lay their hands on the candidate. The bishop then places a stole on his shoulder, and adjusts it. He next anoints his hands with sacred oil, reaches him a chalice containing wine, and a patena with bread, saying, 'RECEIVE POWER TO OFFER SACRI-

FICE TO GOD, AND TO CELEBRATE MASS AS WELL FOR THE LIVING AS FOR THE DEAD.' By these words and ceremonies he is constituted an interpreter and mediator between God and man, the principal function of the priesthood. Finally, placing his hands on the head of the person to be ordained, the bishop says, 'RECEIVE YE THE HOLY GHOST; WHOSE SINS YE SHALL FORGIVE, THEY ARE FORGIVEN THEM; AND WHOSE SINS YE SHALL RETAIN THEY ARE RETAINED. Thus investing him with that divine power of forgiving and retaining sins, which was conferred by our Lord on his disciples. These are the principal and peculiar functions of the priesthood.[12]

These are wonderful pretensions! The apostles themselves claimed no such powers. They never pretended to transform bread and wine into *the body* and blood of our Lord Jesus Christ. There is no record of their claiming to forgive sin, in the place of God, or of pronouncing absolution from sin by his authority. They were to forgive those who sinned against them, but all Christians were to do the same. They laid down *authoritatively* the conditions on which God forgives sin.

Says Dr. Lightfoot: "The Holy Spirit directing them, they were to determine concerning the legal doctrine and practice, being completely instructed and enabled in both by the Holy Spirit descending upon them.

"As to the *persons*, they were endowed with a peculiar gift, so that, the same Spirit directing them, if they would retain and punish the sins of any, a power was delivered into their hands of *delivering* to *Satan*, of punishing with *diseases, plagues*, yea, death *itself*, which Peter did to *Ananias* and *Sapphira*; Paul to *Elymas, Hymeneus* and *Philetus.*"

But the power which the twelve possessed they never assumed to bestow upon others. The record does not show that Christ ever gave them any such power.

Simon Magus was the only one spoken of in the New Testament as ascribing to them such power. And he was most severely rebuked. – Acts 8:18-24.

As to the Romish priests transforming the bread

and wine *into the actual body and blood of the Lord Jesus,* it is a blasphemous assumption. The apostles did not pretend to do any such thing. *For as often as ye eat this bread.* – 1 Cor. 11-26.

Wherefore whosoever shall eat this bread, and drink this cup of the Lord, unworthily, shall be guilty of the body and blood of the Lord. – 27th verse.

They eat unworthily who eat it to satisfy hunger and not to commemorate the sacrificial death of Christ. They do not discern *the Lord's body.*

But whether eaten worthily or unworthily, it is THE BREAD that is eaten.

On the unscriptural view that the Lord's Supper is of the nature of a sacrifice for sin is based the claim that Gospel ministers constitute a *priesthood.* This is an error of the greatest magnitude and fraught with the most direful consequences.

It is remarkable that, though the word *priest* is found in the New Testament one hundred and fifty-one times, *it is never once applied to a Christian minister.* Neither John, nor Peter, nor Paul, nor James is ever called a *priest.*

"What is the reason?"

A *priest* is one who offers sacrifices for the sins of others. "For every high priest taken from among men is ordained for men in things pertaining to God, that he may offer both gifts and sacrifices for sins." – Heb. 5:1. See also Chap. 8:3.

But Christ has offered *himself* a sacrifice for our sins, ONCE FOR ALL. "And every priest standeth daily ministering and offering often times the same sacrifices, which can never take away sins; but this man after he had offered one sacrifice for sins forever, sat down on the right hand of God. – Heb. 10:12. Note well! that THE SACRIFICE FOR SINS IS FOREVER. It is *never to be repeated.*

"For such an high priest became us, who is holy, harmless, undefiled, separate from sinners, and made higher than the heavens; who needeth not daily, as those high priests, to offer up sacrifice, first for his own sins, and then for the people's; for this he did once, when he offered up himself. – Heb. 7:26, 27.

There is then a valid reason why the Christian religion has *no priests. It has no sacrifices for sins to offer.* The sacrifice for sin is complete. The Redeemer has appeared among men. *Man is redeemed.* For ministers to assume to be priests, in the priestly sense, is an open insult to Christ. It is a Heaven-daring usurpation.

The *Christian priesthood* embraces *all* of God's people. It was to *all the saints* that St. Peter wrote: "Ye, also, as lively stones, are built up a spiritual house, an holy priesthood to offer up spiritual sacrifices, acceptable to God by Jesus Christ." – 1 Pet. 2:5.

Also in the 9th verse: "But ye are a chosen generation, a royal priesthood." There is no dispute that all the saints are referred to in both these passages.

The *nature* of these sacrifices is clearly specified. They are –

1. *Our bodies.* "I beseech you, therefore, brethren, by the mercies of God that ye present your bodies a living sacrifice, holy, acceptable unto God, which is your reasonable service." – Rom. 12:1.

No priest is to offer this for another. Each believer in Christ is to offer it for himself.

2. *Good works.* "But to do good and to communicate, forget not; for with such sacrifices God is well pleased." – Heb. 13:16. See also Eph. 5:2.

This direction also is *to all* of God's people.

3. *Praise.* "By him, therefore, let us offer the sacrifice of praise to God continually, that is, the fruit of our lips giving thanks to his name. – Heb. 13:15.

This too is a *sacrifice* that all the saints are to offer. It is not to be done by priest or other proxy. No choir, however skillful, or how highly paid, can relieve us of this duty of offering praise to God.

These are *all* the sacrifices that Christians are directed, in the New Testament, to offer. And each and all of these they are to offer *for themselves.* Not one word is said about offering "the sacrifice of the Mass" as an atonement for our sins. All this is adding to the word of the Lord.

If Christian Ministers were called upon to slaughter cattle and sheep as sacrifices for sin, then it would be improper for women to be ministers. This is the reason why, in the Old Testament, no woman is called a priest. Some of them were *prophets* to instruct and reform the people, but no woman was a priest to offer sacrifices for sins.

In the primitive Christian Church, when the Ministers became proud and aspiring, and assumed priestly prerogatives, they assigned to woman a lower place in the Christian ministry; and finally, as they apostatized more fully, they dropped her from the ministry altogether.

Between these two extremes, of the Friends, who make absolutely nothing of ordination, and of the Romanists, who make an apotheosis, a deification of it, lies the truth.

By Protestants generally, ordination is looked upon as a solemn recognition by the church, of the authority to preach, of those whom God has called to this office, and who have made full proof of their ministry.

John Wesley, referring to ecclesiastics of the Church of England, to which he belonged, said that for forty years he had been in doubt over the question, "What obedience is due to Heathenish priests and mitred infidels?"

So it is quite evident that he did not regard ordination as bestowing a Christian, much less an angelic or godlike character.

Ordination is necessary to prevent improper persons from thrusting themselves into the ministry, and thus bringing the Gospel into contempt. Daniel Webster said; "Forms are as necessary as hoops on a barrel; they keep the whole from falling to pieces."

"The essential elements of the act of ordination," says Rev. H. J. Van Dyke, Sr., D. D., "are *prayer, and the laying on of hands, with the avowed intention of set-*

ting apart the candidate to the work of the ministry, as one who, after due examination, is believed to be called of God to that office."[13]

For ordination there is the plain authority of the New Testament.

"*The Ordination of the Seven Deacons*"[14] This marked event in the history of the Church occurred in immediate sequence of the outpouring of the Holy Ghost at the Pentecost, and from the space allotted to it in the sacred record (Acts 6:2-6), as well as from the fact that all the apostles were present, it may now be considered, as it doubtless was during the whole apostolic period, a model ordination for the subsequent Church. Its characteristic features were: (1.) A demand for men of honest report, full of the Holy Ghost and wisdom; (2.) An election or choice by the church on that basis; (3.) Prayer by the apostles; (4.) The laying on of hands, presumably, by several of the apostles, as representative of the whole body. In this act the apostles illustrated their ideas of the proper functions of the church in reference to its future ministers, and established a precedent, of perpetual authority. It was a precedent, moreover, in obvious harmony with the precept of our Lord, given in connection with his appointment of the seventy (Luke 10:2), "Pray ye, therefore, the Lord of the harvest, that he would send forth laborers into his harvest." The apostles evidently regarded this as the standing commission and perpetual duty of the church, in reference to the promotion of Christ's Kingdom in the earth. In it they saw that the Lord claimed the work of evangelizing the world as his own, and also the prerogative of calling and sending forth laborers, while at the same time, he charged the church with the responsibility of prayer and co-operation. This, too, was in harmony with the Saviour's promised gift of the Holy Ghost as the guide of the church when he should no longer be present as its visible head. The Spirit's influence was specially promised in answer to prayer, and it was only a praying church endowed with the Holy Ghost that could become the light of the world, and the agency of its salvation. So long as the church illustrated these characteristics, it gloriously fulfilled its mission. It grew rapidly by the addition of regenerated believers, many of whom, in proportion to the demands of its widening work, were called of God, and moved of the Holy Ghost to preach to others the same Gospel that had become to them the power of God unto salvation. The function of the church, therefore, as to ordination was, not to create or bestow the gift of the ministry, but simply to recognize and authenticate it when bestowed by the Head of the Church."

The ordination of elders. In the Apostolic Church, Bishops and Elders were the same. "And from Miletus he sent to Ephesus, and called the elders of the church." When they **were** come together he said to them; "Take heed, **there**fore, unto yourselves, and to all the flock over the **which** the Holy Ghost hath made you overseers, to **feed** the church of God, which he hath purchased with his own blood."– Acts 20:17, 28. The word here translated overseer is, in the original, *episcopos, bishop.* From this we learn – 1. That those having the oversight of the Church were called *elders* or *bishops.* These two words were used interchangeably. 2. That preaching was the chief business of these elders or bishops. They were made bishops by the Holy Ghost that they might FEED *the church of God.*

So, in the various lists that are given us in the New Testament, of the officers of the church, elders and bishops are never both found in the same list. These elders were ordained. "And when they had ordained them elders in every church, and had prayed with fasting, they commended them to the Lord, on whom they believed." – Acts 14:23.

"For this cause left I thee in Crete, that thou shouldest set in order the things that are wanting, and ordain elders in every city as I had appointed thee. If any be blameless, the husband of one wife, having faithful children not accused of riot or unruly. For a bishop must be blameless – Titus 1:5-7.

It is evident that those whom he calls elders in the fifth verse he calls bishops in the seventh.

We see also that the Apostolic churches were not independent, but the same men had official oversight of many churches.

Ordaining Apostles. "Now there were in the church that was at Antioch certain prophets and teachers; as Barnabas and Simeon that was called Niger, and Lucius of Cyrene, and Manaen, which had been brought up with Herod the tetrarch and Saul.

"And as they ministered to the Lord and fasted, the Holy Ghost said, Separate me Barnabas and Saul for the work whereunto I have called them.

"And when they had fasted and prayed, and laid their hands on them they sent them away." – Acts 13:1-3.

"The events above narrated," say McClintock and Strong, "occurred some two years after the commission of Saul of Tarsus, following which 'straightway he preached Christ in the synagogues' – Acts 9, 20. Becoming associated with Barnabas, he also 'spake boldly in the name of the Lord Jesus' at Jerusalem. Both these men seem to have labored as evangelists whenever they had opportunity, and their ministry, having been given of God, was honored by his blessing. They were now called to higher responsibilities. 'They were to go forth under the sanction of the church and not only to proclaim the truth, but also to baptize converts, to organize Christian congregations, and to ordain Christian ministers. It was therefore proper that, on this occasion, they should be regularly invested with the ecclesiastical commission. In the circumstantial record of this proceeding, in the Acts of the Apostles, we have a proof of the wisdom of the Author of Revelation. He foresaw that the rite of the laying on of hands would be sadly abused; that it would be represented as possessing something like a magic potency; and that it would at length be con-

verted by a small class of ministers, into an ecclesiastical monopoly. He has therefore supplied us with an
antidote against delusion by permitting us, in this
simple narrative, to scan its exact import. And what
was the virtue of the ordination here described? Did
it furnish Paul and Barnabas with a title to the ministry? Not at all. God himself had already called them
to the work, and they could receive no higher autho-
rization. Did it necessarily add anything to the elo-
quence, or the prudence, or the knowledge, or the
piety of the missionaries? No results of the kind
could be produced by any such ceremony. What,
then, was its meaning? The evangelist himself furnishes an answer. The Holy Ghost required that
Barnabas and Saul should be *separated* to the work to
which the Lord had called them, and the laying on of
hands was the *mode* or *form* in which they were set
apart or designated to the office. This rite to an Israel-
ite, suggested grave and hallowed associations. When
a Jewish father invoked a benediction on any of his
family, he laid his hand upon the head of the child;
when a Jewish priest devoted an animal in sacrifice,
he laid his hand upon the head of the victim; and
when a Jewish rabbi invested another with office, he
laid his hand upon the head of the new functionary.
The ordination of these brethren possessed all this
significance. By the laying on of hands the ministers
of Antioch implored a blessing upon Barnabas and
Saul, and announced their separation or dedication to
the work of the gospel and intimated their investiture
with ecclesiastical authority.' "[15]

There is nothing, then, in the nature of ordination
which indicates that no woman should ever be ordained. If she is *called of God* to his work, and this is
evident to the church, then may the church *separate*
her to this work by ordination.

Ordination, while it does not, *in the rite itself*, con-
vey any supernatural, or magical power, yet it should
be the occasion of great and permanent blessing to

the person ordained. But this depends, not upon the form, but upon the parties concerned. If those ordaining are proud, and worldly, and carnal, and formal, and the candidate is unconverted, ordination, in all probability, will only make him more proud, exacting and aspiring. But if those who ordain, are men *full of faith and of the Holy Ghost*, and the one ordained is spiritual, humble and fully consecrated to God, he may receive at his ordination such a baptism of the spirit as shall give him new power all the rest of his days.

"God knows," says Whitfield, "how deep a concern entering into the ministry and preaching was to me. I have prayed a thousand times till the sweat has dropped from my face like rain, that God, of his infinite mercy, would not let me enter into the church, till he called me to and thrust me forth in his work. I said, Lord I cannot go. I shall be puffed up with pride, and fall into the condemnation of the devil. Lord, do not let me go yet. I pleaded to be at Oxford two or three years more. I intended to make one hundred and fifty sermons, and thought that I would set up with a good stock in trade. I remember praying, wrestling and striving with God. I said, I am undone. I am unfit to preach in thy great name. Send me not, Lord – send me not yet. I wrote to all my friends in town and country to pray against the bishop's solicitation, but they insisted I should go into orders before I was twenty-two. After all their solicitations these words came into my mind: 'Nothing shall pluck you out of my hands'; they came warm to my heart. Then, and not till then, I said, Lord I *will* go; send me when thou wilt." He was ordained; and he said: "When the bishop laid his hands upon my head, my heart was melted down, and I offered up my whole spirit and soul and body."

Complaint was made to the bishop that, by his first sermon he drove fifteen mad. The good man replied that he hoped their madness would last.

CHAPTER V.

OBJECTIONS – OLD TESTAMENT.

"God made all his creatures free;
Life itself is liberty;
God ordained no other bands
Than united hearts and hands."
— *James Montgomery.*

THE objections to the ordination of women may be classed under two heads – *Scriptural* and *natural.*

It is urged that the Bible represents the woman as inferior to the man, and subject to him; therefore she should not be permitted to occupy a position equal to his, either in church or in state. As proof of this, the fact that she was created last is presented.

But, if this proves anything, it proves her superiority. For the work of creation proceeded in regular gradation from the lower to the higher.

Matter is not eternal. Away back *in the beginning,* millions of millions of years before our earth was fitted up for the abode of man, *God created the heaven and the earth.*

On the first of our six days of creation, light appeared. On the second, the atmosphere was formed. On the third day, the waters of the earth were gathered together, the dry land appeared, and our vegetable world was brought into existence.

On the fourth day, light was concentrated around the sun, and it was made a luminous body, and the celestial luminaries were so arranged as to afford an accurate measurement of time, and to give distinction to the seasons.

On the fifth day, fish, fowls and reptiles were created.

On the sixth day, land animals were created – man last – the male first – the woman last of all.

Mathew Henry, in his comment on this verse, says: "That Adam was first formed, then Eve (1 Tim. 2:13), and she was made *of* the man and *for* the man (1 Cor. 11:8, 9), all which is urged there as reasons for the humility, modesty, silence and submissiveness of that sex in general, and particularly the subjection and reverence which wives owe to their own husbands. Yet man being made last of the creatures, as the best and most excellent of all, Eve's, being made *after* Adam, and *out* of him, puts an honor upon that sex, as the glory of the man. – 1 Cor. 11:7. If man is the head, she is the crown; a crown to her husband, the crown of the visible creation. The man was dust refined, but the woman was dust double refined, one remove further from the earth."

Woman was created, not as the *servant* of man, but as his *companion,* his *equal.* "And the Lord God said: It is not good that the man should be alone; I will make him an help meet for him." – Gen. 2:18.

Dr. Adam Clarke, in his comment on this verse, says: *"I will make him a help meet for him; ezer kenegedo,* a help, a counterpart of himself, one formed from him, and a perfect resemblance of his person. If the word be rendered scrupulously literally, it signifies one *like,* or *as himself,* standing *opposite to* or *before him.* And this implies that the woman was to be a perfect resemblance of the man, possessing neither inferiority nor superiority, but being in all things *like* and *equal* to himself."

The *dominion* which God gave to man at the creation was a *joint* dominion. It was given to the woman equally as to the man.

"And God said: Let us make man in our image, after our likeness; and let them have dominion over the fish of the sea, and over the fowl of the air, and over the cattle, and over all the earth, and over every creeping thing that creepeth upon the earth.

"So God created man in his own image, in the image
of God created he him; male and female created he
them." – Gen. 1:26, 27.

*Let*THEM *have dominion.*

It is, then, evident that God created woman a *female man* – nothing more – nothing less. She had all
the rights and prerogatives of the man. The dominion
given to him was given equally to her.

Nothing was said of the subjection of woman before the fall. After that sad event, it was said to the
woman, as a part of her punishment: "Thy desire
shall be to thy husband and he shall rule over thee." –
Gen. 3:16.

On this verse Dr. Adam Clarke says, "*And he shall
rule over thee,* though at their creation both were
formed with equal rights, and the woman had probably as much right to *rule* as the man; but subjection
to the will of her husband is one part of her curse;
and so very capricious is this *will* often, that a sorer
punishment no human being can well have, to be at
all in a state of liberty, and under the protection of
wise and equal laws."

But it was promised that "The seed of the woman
should bruise the serpent's head." – Gen. 3:15. Christ
was THE SEED OF THE WOMAN. Woman gave to
the world man's Redeemer. If she was first in the fall,
she was first in the restoration. *Christ hath redeemed us
from the curse of the law, being made a curse for us.* – Gal.
3:13. The US includes *woman.*

The Pharisees asked Christ: "Is it lawful for a man
to put away his wife for every cause?"

In his answer he did not appeal to existing laws,
or long established customs. He based his answer on
the *state of things that existed before the fall.* "Have ye
not read, that he which made them at the beginning,
made them male and female?" – Matt. 19:4. Why this
appeal to *the beginning*? IT WAS TO RE-ENACT THE
LAW ENACTED THEN. *For this cause shall a man leave*

father and mother, and shall cleave to his wife; and they twain shall be one flesh. Thus Christ *restored the primitive law.* He said nothing about the *subjection of woman –not one word.*

"But," it is objected, "domestic society requires the wife to be subject to the husband."

This is a great mistake. If it did, Christ would doubtless have given directions accordingly.

But it does not. The greatest domestic happiness always exists where husband and wife live together on terms of equality. Two men, having individual interests, united only by business ties, daily associate as partners for years, without either of them being in subjection to the other. They consider each other as equals; and treat each other as equals. Then, cannot a man and woman, united by conjugal love, the strongest tie that can unite two human beings, having *the same* interests, live together in the same manner?

Christ came to repair the ruin wrought by the fall. In Him, and in Him only, is Paradise *restored.*

The Gospel belongs to woman as much as to man.

But, it is again objected that under the Aaronic priesthood men only were priests.

This is true; but the priests were not the only or the chief religious teachers of the Jews. The prophets ranked in this respect above the priests.

But women prophesied. Miriam, was a prophetess – Ex. 15:20. And God in speaking of the deliverance of his people from Egypt, classes her with Moses and Aaron. "And I sent before thee Moses, Aaron and Miriam." – Micah 6:4. She was, then, one of the chosen leaders of his people sent by God. Does not this answer the question, Why did not God appoint a woman to be a leader, if it is ever right for a woman to lead? With Moses and Aaron God sent Miriam "before" His people – that is to lead them.

Deborah was a prophetess and a judge. She performed all the duties that men did who judged Israel, even, to leading their armies to successful battle – Judges 4:4. Huldah was a prophetess (2 Ki. 22:14);

and so was Noadiah. Nah. 6:14.

Then we conclude that there is nothing in the creation of woman or in her condition under the law which proves that no woman should be ordained as a minister of the Gospel.

CHAPTER VI.

OBJECTIONS – NEW TESTAMENT

"All mystery is defect, and cloudy words
   Are feebleness, not strength; are loss, not gain;
Men win no victories with spectre swords;
   The phantom barque plows the broad sea in vain."
                                                    – *Bonar.*

IN all that we have heard and read against the right of woman to be, in the fullest sense, a minister of the Gospel, we have never heard or read a single quotation from the words of Jesus against this right. This is significant. Christ applied the same rules of moral conduct to the woman as to the man. His treatment of the woman taken in adultery has scarcely a parallel. No woman ever came to him to be repulsed.

But, it is said, if women are to preach, why did he not choose a woman among the twelve?

We ask, in reply, if *gentiles* are to preach, why did he not choose a *gentile* among the twelve? Why were the twelve *Jews, every* one of them? The example is as binding in the one case as the other.

But, it is answered, Paul settles the question. *"There is neither Jew nor Greek, there is neither bond nor free, there is neither male nor female; for ye are all one in Christ Jesus."* – Gal. 3:28. It is contrary to all sound principles of interpretation to say that this passage accords to a Greek the same rights in the Gospel that it does to a Jew, in *one sense*, and to a *woman* the same rights that it does to a *man* in *another*, and much more *restricted sense*.

If this gives to *men* of all nations the right to become ministers of the Gospel, it gives to *women* precisely the same right.

Make this the KEY TEXT upon this subject, and give to other passages such a construction as will make them agree with it, and all is harmony. The apparent conflict is at an end. The fetters are taken off from woman, and she is left free to serve Christ in any position she may be qualified and called to fill. Why should not this be done?

It is objected, in the strong, clear language of an able minister: "In what are male and female *one* in Christ Jesus? Certainly not in every respect. There is nothing in the context by which you can come to the conclusion that Paul is here laying down an abstract principle, applicable outside the limits of the subject under discussion. Now what is that subject? Is it not the one that runs through the entire epistle and especially through the chapter of which the verse in questions forms a part? viz: That all men, Jews and Gentiles alike, are saved by faith, and not by the works of the law, according to the covenant of God made with Abraham. From first to last there is no other subject introduced or considered in this chapter. And therefore fairness of interpretation requires us to understand the teaching of the 28th verse to be simply this: In the matter of salvation all are one. The male is saved by faith. The female is saved by faith. The Jew is saved by faith and also the Greek. Likewise the bondman and the freeman. In this respect, all are one, being baptized into Jesus Christ, they become equally children of God, saved by faith alone. To carry this idea of *oneness* further is to bring into the text what is not there, and add to the inspired word."[16]

To this objection we reply:

1. If this verse referred *only to salvation by* faith, the *female* would not be specified. It would be a superfluity. As we have seen, woman is a *female man.*[17] *In the many offers of salvation made in the New Testament, woman* is not *specially* mentioned. *Not once.* "He that believeth and is baptized shall be saved," in-

cludes woman as well as man. Every one so understood it. There was no dispute about it. So, in the first prayer meeting, it appears the women went ahead. "These all continued, with one accord, in prayer and supplication *with the women.* – Acts 1:14. Women believed in Christ. "And believers were the more added to the Lord multitudes, both of *men and women.* "– Acts 5:14. They were so active in his cause as to provoke persecution. "Saul, hailing men and *women committed them to prison.*" – Acts 8:3. Though, in the Jewish church, the males only received the sign of the covenant, yet in the Christian church, women were, from the first, baptized. "*They* were baptized, both *men and women.*" – Acts 8:12. Yet there is no specific command to baptize *women,* nor any *separate* offer of salvation to them. So, if Gal. 3:28 referred to salvation alone, the female would not have been mentioned in it. The "Greek" and the "bond" might have been mentioned with propriety. For it took a miracle to convince Peter that a Greek, or Gentile, could be saved by Christ. But it would have stopped with them. All regarded women as included in the general provisions of the Gospel for the salvation of mankind.

So we must give this verse its full, natural, comprehensive, broad meaning. We must understand it to teach, as it actually does, the perfect equality of all, under the Gospel, in *rights* and *privileges,* without respect to *nationality,* or condition, or sex.

2. There are two correct modes of reasoning:

(1.) From particulars to deduce a general truth.

(2.) From a general, admitted truth, or axiom, make an application to particulars.

The apostle here adopts the first method. He shows that Abraham was justified by faith; that the Mosaic law was temporary, to last only till Christ came; that all who have faith in Christ become the children of God.

Then he makes two general statements –

1. That in Christ Jesus all *peculiar* privileges based on *nationality,* or *condition,* or *sex are abolished.* In the Gospel one nation has the *same* rights and privileges as *another,* the bond the same as the *free,* the *female* the same as the *male.*

2. That all, without distinction, who believe in Christ, are the children of Abraham and heirs according to the promise.

With this agrees Dr. Adam Clarke in his comment on this verse. *"Neither male nor female.* With great reason the apostle introduces this. Between the privileges of *men* and *women* there was a great disparity among the Jews. A *man* might shave his head, and rend his clothes in the time of mourning; a *woman* was not permitted to do so. A *man* might impose the vow of *nasirate* upon his son; a woman could not do this on her daughter. A *man* might be shorn on account of the *nasirate* of his father; a woman could not. A *man* might betroth his daughter; a *woman* had no such power. A *man* might sell his daughter; a *woman* could not. In many cases they were treated more like *children* than *adults;* and to this day are not permitted to assemble with the men in the synagogues, but are put up in galleries, where they can scarcely see, nor can they be seen. Under the blessed spirit of Christianity they have equal *rights,* equal *privileges,* and equal blessings, and, let me add, they are equally *useful."*

This is all we contend for. We are in full agreement with these words of the great commentator.

Again, it is urged that Paul in express words forbids women to become ministers of the Gospel. In proof of this, two passages are quoted:

"Let your women keep silence in the churches; for it is not permitted unto them to speak; but they are commanded to be under obedience, as also saith the law. And if they will learn anything let them ask their husbands at home; for it is a shame for women to speak in the church." – 1 Cor. 14:34, 35.

"Let the woman learn in silence with all subjection. But I suffer not a woman to teach, nor to usurp authority over the man, but to be in silence." – 1 Tim. 2:11, 12.

1. These are the only passages of the kind in the Bible. There are no others that seem to forbid woman to preach, or to perform all the other duties of a minister of the Gospel.

2. No denomination applies these passages *literally*. If they did, they would not allow:

(1.) Women to sing in church. For to sing is not to *keep silence*.

(2.) Nor to pray; for the same reason.

(3.) Nor to testify; for to testify is to *speak*.

(4.) Nor to teach in the Sabbath school or elsewhere; for the statement is general – *I suffer not a woman to teach*.

(5.) Nor to write religious books, or for religious periodicals; for this is to *teach*.

Notice. *Preaching is not specified.* It is forbidden only as it is one method of *breaking the silence*, one mode of *teaching*. So far, then, all are agreed that these words of Paul are not to be taken *literally*. The most rigid Presbyterians allow women to sing in the church, and to teach in the Sabbath school.

Madame Guyon, and other holy women among the Roman Catholics, have written religious books, and so have taught.

3. It is evident that Paul did not intend to prohibit women from taking any part in religious services, or even from preaching. For, *in this same epistle,* he gives directions about their dress when in public congregations they take a part in the exercises, – pray and prophesy – that is, preach.

"But every woman that prayeth or prophesieth with her head uncovered dishonoreth her head; for that is even all one as if she were shaven." – 1 Cor. 11:5.

This certainly assumes that she was to pray and prophesy in public.

Then Paul did not require all women to *keep silence* in the church, in an *absolute sense*. He did permit some women *to teach*, for unless they taught how could they *edify* their hearers? He would have them so dress as not to excite the suspicion that they were not modest women.

Priscilla was a woman. Apollos was an eloquent preacher of the Gospel. But Aquila and Priscilla expounded unto Apollos the way of God more perfectly.

Paul, in his epistles, sent his salutations to several women who *labored in the Lord.* "And I entreat thee also, true yoke-fellow, help those women which labored with me in the Gospel, with Clement, also, and with other my fellow laborers, whose names are in the book of life." – Phil. 4:3. The word here translated *labored with,* is συ νήθλησάν, sunethlesan, from sun, together, and athleo, to strive, the word from which is derived our word *athletic.* It means to *strive along with one, on his side, to help vigorously.*

Clement was a celebrated minister, the same, it is supposed, who was afterwards bishop of Rome. These women gave Paul the same assistance that Clement did.

"Greet Priscilla and Aquila, my helpers in Christ Jesus; who have for my life laid down their own necks; unto whom not only I give thanks, but also all the churches of the Gentiles."

Helpers, συ ν ε ρ γ ούς, sunergous, *fellow workers.* It seems that they not only labored *with the apostle,* but incurred such perils for his sake as secured for them the thanks of all the Gentile churches.

With others, he salutes Mary, Junia and Julia.

"Salute Tryphena and Tryphosa, who labor in the Lord. Salute the beloved Persis, which labored much in the Lord." – Rom. 16:12.

In his comments on this verse, Dr. Clarke says: "We learn from this, that Christian *women,* as well as *men,* labored in the ministry of the word.

"Many have spent much useless labor in endeavoring to prove that these women did not *preach*. That there were some *prophetesses* as well as *prophets* in the Christian church, we learn; and that a *woman* might *pray* or *prophesy,* provided she had her *head covered*, we know; and that whoever *prophesied* spoke unto others to *edification, exhortation* and comfort, St. Paul declares. – 1 Cor. 14:3. And that no preacher can do *more*, every person must acknowledge; because to *edify, exhort* and *comfort* are the prime ends of the Gospel ministry. If *women* thus *prophesied,* then women *preached.* There is, however, much more than this implied in the Christian ministry, of which men only, and men called of God, are capable."

In this last sentence we see the power of prejudice even over so great and good a man as Dr. Clarke. What this "much more" is, of which "men only are capable," he fails to tell us, and we are at a loss to imagine.

St. Paul himself then makes it clear that the two verses quoted above, in which he appears to forbid, in general terms, women to *speak* in meeting, or to *teach,* either *in meeting or out,* are not to be construed literally.

4. Peter says that in all of Paul's epistles *are some things hard to be understood.* – 2 Pet. 3:15. Why not class among these things *hard to be understood,* what he says about women keeping silence in the churches, and conform our practice to what we find, in other passages, that women actually did in the apostolic church? We can see nothing wrong in such a course. Some churches that do not allow women to pray or testify in their public meetings, and others that permit her to go thus far, but do not allow her equal rights in the church with a man, pay no attention whatever to the prohibition of women to adorn themselves in *gold, or pearls, or costly array.* – 1 Tim. 2:9.

Yet the whole tenor of Scripture is in harmony with the latter restriction!

5. But we think what he says about women

keeping silence in the church may be satisfactorily explained.

The connection in 1 Cor. 14:34 shows that the Apostle is speaking of *disorder* and *confusion,* and not of the right of women to preach. "For God is not the author of confusion." – v. 33.

The man is commanded to *be silent* under certain circumstances. *But if there be no interpreter let him keep silence in the church.* – v. 28.

Is the woman to be in subjection to proper authority? So is the man. *And the spirits of the prophets are subject to the prophets.* – v. 32.

Chrysostom, who lived in the fourth century, in his comment on 1 Cor. 14:34 throws light upon this subject.

"Having abated the disturbance both from the tongues, and from the prophesyings; and having made a law to prevent confusion, that they who prophesy should be silent when another begins; he next in course proceeds to the disorder which arose from the women, rooting out their unseasonable boldness of speech; and that very opportunely. For if to them that have the gifts it is not permitted to speak inconsiderately, nor when they will, and this though they be moved by the Spirit; much less to those women who prate idly and to no purpose. Therefore he represses their babbling and that with much authority, and taking the law along with him, thus he sews up their mouths; not simply exhorting here, or giving counsel, but he even laying his commands on them vehemently, by the recitation of an ancient law on that subject. For having said, "Let your women keep silence in the churches; and, it is not permitted unto them to speak but to be under obedience, he added, as also saith the law. And where does the law say this? (Thy desire shall be to thy husband and he shall rule over thee.)"

Again, speaking of the behavior of women in the church, Chrysostom says: "There is apt to be great noise among them – much clamor, and talking, and nowhere so much as in this place. They may all be seen here talking more than in the market, or at the bath. For, as if they came hither for recreation, they are all engaged in conversing upon unprofitable subjects. Thus all is confusion."

The city of Corinth was the Paris of its day. The people were gay, giddy, devoted to pleasure. The Christian church in that city was composed of such of this people as had accepted Christ. The women admitted to the liberty of the Gospel, *abused* this liberty as the men also did. The larger part of this 14th chapter of 1 Corinthians is devoted to regulations for the men. When he speaks of women, it is, not in general terms, but *your women,* – the women that yield to the disorderly spirit that prevails among you. The prohibition (in the 34th verse) was local and temporary.

Timothy was laboring among churches composed chiefly of converts from heathenism. So when Paul says in his epistle to Timothy: "I suffer not a woman to teach, nor to usurp authority over the man, but to be in silence," the words are evidently used in the same meaning as the similar words in Corinthians: When a woman is properly authorized to teach she does not *usurp authority.* The authority duly given her she has a right to exercise in a proper manner and within the proper limits.

We conclude this chapter with a saying that all must admit. The restrictions which we have been considering stand just as much in the way of a woman's doing what the churches generally permit her to do – sing, or pray, or speak as they do in the way of her ordination.

We must either go back or we must go ahead. We must either give her equal rights with men or we must reduce her to the servitude of by-gone ages. Either we must be governed by the Christian law of love and equity, or we must take a step back into barbarism and be governed by the law of brute force. Which shall it be?

The present position of the churches is not only

wrong, but inconsistent. They concede to woman too much, if Paul's words restricting her are taken literally; they concede too little, if these words are to be so understood as to harmonize with the rest of the Bible.

"Now, shame upon ye, parish Popes!
Was't thus with those your predecessors,
Who sealed with racks and fire and ropes
Their loving kindness to transgressors?"
— *Whittier.*

If woman, in using her voice, in praising God, or declaring His truth, in your churches, is a transgressor, then silence her at whatever cost; if she is doing right then remove all shackles and give her the liberty of the Gospel.

CHAPTER VII.

OBJECTIONS – NATURAL.

"In the still air the music lies unheard;
    In the rough marble beauty hides unseen;
To wake the music and the beauty, needs
    The master's touch, the sculptor's chisel keen."

                                                    – Bonar.

IT is objected that a woman in the pulpit is out of her place; that nature never designed her to be a minister of the Gospel.

With classical literature, the old heathen ideas about woman's true position have come down to us.

Aristotle said: "The relation of man to woman is that of the governor to his subject."

It is urged that woman is naturally unfitted for the duties of a minister of the Gospel; that Nature by its inexorable laws stands in the way of her ordination; that she is physically disqualified for the ministerial office.

If this is so then there is not the slightest necessity for closing the pulpit against her. It requires no legislation to keep sheep from plunging into the river, or fish from invading the land.

"One thing we may be certain of," says John Stuart Mill, "that what is contrary to women's nature to do, they will never be made to do by simply giving their nature free play. The anxiety of mankind to interfere in behalf of nature, for fear lest nature should not succeed in effecting its purpose, is an altogether unnecessary solicitude. What women by nature cannot do it is quite superfluous to forbid them from

49

doing. What they can do, but not so well as the men who are their competitors, competition suffices to exclude them from; since nobody asks for protective duties and bounties in favor of women; it is only asked that the present bounties and protective duties in favor of men should be recalled. If women have a greater natural inclination for some things than for others, there is no need of laws or social inculcation to make the majority of them do the former in preference to the latter.

"Whatever women's services are most wanted for, the free play of competition will hold out the strongest inducements to them to undertake. And, as the words imply, they are most wanted for the thing for which they are most fit; by the apportionment of which to them the collective faculties of the two sexes can be applied on the whole with the greatest sum of valuable result."[18]

No special legislation, either by church or state, is needed to give to women their proper place. Leave them as free as the men are, and they will instinctively find their true place. If a woman's true position is that of wife, she will not hesitate to accept it if the right man makes the offer. But there are more women than men in the United States. Why may not some of these become ministers of the Gospel if God calls them to the position and they are duly qualified for it?

That some women possess the physical ability to preach is no longer a question; it is a demonstrated fact that they have this ability, for some women do preach, and do successfully the most exhaustive labors of a preacher – hold protracted meetings.

What does an ordained preacher do that is a greater draft upon the physical powers than preaching, and especially holding revival services? Some women have engaged in callings that tax the physical powers more than preaching and administering the sacraments.

They are successful physicians and lawyers.
Lowell, one of our popular American poets, writes:

"They talk about a woman's sphere
    As though it had a limit;
There's not a spot in earth or heaven,
There's not a task to mankind given
    Without a woman in it."

The vocation of a soldier would seem to be one
for which women are specially unfitted by nature. Yet
whenever they have undertaken it, they have met
with, at least, the average success of the men.

Deborah won more honor than Barak in the battle
which they fought under her direction.

In the battle fought by Xerxes against the Greeks,
which decided the destiny of Europe, the only branch
of his army that drove the enemy, was that commanded by Artemisia, queen of Halicarnassus.
Herodotus, styled the father of History, speaks of an
army of female warriors, called "Amazons," who
were by no means deficient in the qualities of good
soldiers. After they settled down, he says, they "retained their ancient mode of living, both going out on
horseback to hunt with their husbands and without
their husbands, and joining in war, and wearing the
same dress as the men."[19] By their rules "no virgin
was permitted to marry till she had killed an enemy."

The Athenians based their claims to precedence
over the other tribes of Greece, among other things,
on the fact that they "performed a valiant exploit
against the Amazons, who once made an irruption
into Attica from the river Thermidon."[20]

It was a Greek Amazon of more recent date that
the poet, Bryant, represents as singing:

"I buckle to my slender side
    The pistol and the scimitar,
And in my maiden flower and pride
    Am come to share the tasks of war.
And yonder stands my fiery steed,
    That paws the ground, and neighs to go,
My charger of the Arab breed, –
    I took him from the routed foe."

Stanley speaks of the Amazons of the King of Uganda, and says: "What strikes us most is the effect of discipline."[21]

During the Hundred Years' war between France and England there came a time when it seemed as if France must perish from among the nations. The English had possession of most of the large cities. The French King, Charles VI. had died, and the Parliament of Paris had recognized Henry VI. of England as "King of England and France." The rightful heir to the French throne was regarded as an indolent and frivolous prince. What remained of the French army was disheartened and demoralized. Orleans, the chief city still in possession of the French, was closely besieged by a powerful army.

At this juncture a peasant girl of sixteen announced that she was called of God to deliver the kingdom. She was unlettered, modest, industrious, and deeply pious. Her neighbors believed and respected her. To one of the French Knights who went to see her, as she was trying to find someone to take her to the King, she said: "Assuredly, I would far rather be spinning beside my poor mother; for this other is not my condition; but I must go and do the work because my Lord wills that I should do it."

"Who is your Lord?" demanded the knight.

"The Lord God," replied the maid.

"By my faith," said the knight, "I will take you to the King, God helping."

She was furnished with a coat of mail, a lance, a sword, and a horse – in short with the complete equipment of a man-at-arms.

She rode on horseback four hundred and fifty miles, with a suitable escort, in eleven days, through a country, occupied here and there by the English, and everywhere a theatre of war.

The King received her, though some of his offices were greatly displeased at seeing more confidence placed in a peasant girl than in experienced warriors. She was examined by the Chancellor of France, the archbishop of Rheims, five bishops, the King's counsellors, and several learned doctors. The examination lasted a fortnight. Addressing one of them, a learned doctor, she said:

"I know not A. nor B.; but in our Lord's Book there is more than in your books; I come on behalf of the King of Heaven to cause the siege of Orleans to be raised, and to take the King to Rheims that he may be crowned and anointed there."

The doctors decided in Joan's favor.

They reported that, "After a grave inquiry there had been discovered in her nought but goodness, humility, devotion, honesty, simplicity. Before Orleans she professes to be going to show her sign; so she must be taken to Orleans; for to give her up without any appearance of evil on her part would be to fight against the Holy Spirit, and to become unworthy of aid from God."

She was then examined by three of the greatest ladies of the Kingdom as to her life as a woman. They found in her "nothing but truth, virtue and modesty." "She spoke to them," says the chronicle, "with such sweetness and grace that she drew tears from their eyes."

She excused herself to them for the dress she wore, though the sternest doctors had not reproached her for it. "It is more decent," said the archbishop of Embrun "to do such things in man's dress, since they must be done along with men."

She went to Orleans at the head of a small but enthusiastic band of troops.

The population received her with "joy as great as if they had seen God come down among them." "They felt," says the journal of the siege, "all of them recomforted and, as it were, disbesieged by the divine virtue which they had been told existed in this simple maid."

The English were defiant. To her summons to depart and return to their own country they replied with coarse insults. A fierce battle was fought. Joan placed a scaling ladder against a rampart and was the first to mount. She was wounded between the neck and shoulder. She felt faint, but prayed, and pulled out the arrow with her own hand. A dressing of oil was applied to the wound, and she retired and was continually in prayer.

The French were becoming tired and discouraged, and showed signs of retreating. She resumed her arms, mounted her horse, waved her banner, and rushed forward to the battle. The French took courage, the English were struck with consternation and fled. The next day they retreated and the siege of Orleans was raised.

In many other movements Joan was successful. At length the King, Charles VII., of France was crowned at Rheims.

"Anger is cruel and wrath is outrageous, but who can stand before envy?"

Many in authority who should have been her friends, secretly plotted against her, so that her counsels were disregarded, and at last she was betrayed into the hands of the English, who burned her alive at the stake. She met fate with the same heroic devotion that had characterized her life. Two of the Judges who had condemned her to that cruel death, as she ceased to live cried out: "Would that my soul were where I believe the soul of that woman is."

And the Secretary of the King of England, on returning from the execution, said: "We are all lost: we have burned a saint."

It is true this is an extraordinary case.

But who shall say that, in these days, when the world has so nearly led the church into captivity that God would not, if his spirit could have free course, raise up matrons and maidens to drive back the hosts of hell, and lead on the army of believers to glorious victories?

On whatever shoulders God is pleased to place the epaulettes man should not dare pull them off.

All these examples certainly prove that some

women may possess the physical strength and endurance, and the courage to discharge all the duties of an ordained minister of the Gospel.

CHAPTER VIII.

WOMEN APOSTLES.

"How ready is the man to go
Whom God hath never sent!
How timorous, diffident and slow
His chosen instrument."

—Charles Wesley.

"Thus have ye made the commandment of God of none effect by your tradition."—Jesus.

IT is assumed that there were but twelve apostles, and that the apostolical office expired with them. Nothing can be plainer than that the New Testament teaches the contrary. "And God hath set some in the church, first apostles, secondarily prophets, thirdly teachers, after that miracles, then gifts of healings, helps, governments, diversities of tongues." – 1 Cor. 12:28.

This language implies, not a temporary provision, but a permanent arrangement.

While the twelve are spoken of in the Gospel, by way of pre-eminence, as *the apostles,* yet other apostles are mentioned in the New Testament.

Thus Matthias, who was chosen to succeed Judas, is called an apostle (Acts 1:26); so are Paul and Barnabas (Acts 14:14); and so is Epaphroditus (Phil. 2:25), *messenger* in our version, but *apostle* in the original; the brethren to whom Paul refers in 2 Cor. 8:23; and Andronicus and Junia, Rom. 16:7. All these in the original are called apostles.

So strong are the prejudices of even our most candid commentators that they resort to every expedient known to criticism in order so to explain this striking text (Rom. 16:7) that it will not prove that a woman was an apostle. It seems impossible to them that a woman was an apostle in the apostolic church: and they therefore feel obliged to explain away the plain declaration of Paul that Junia was an apostle.

1. They raise the question whether Junia was a woman.

Adam Clarke says: "*Junia* may probably be the name of a woman."

Dean Alford, who is usually so fair, says: " Ι ο υ ν ι ά, may be fem. from Ι ο υ ν ι α (junia), in which case she is probably the wife of Andronicus, – or masc, from Ι ο υ ν ι άς (Junianus contr. Junias)."

It is very significant that neither Dean Alford nor Dr. Clarke gives any reason for the doubt they suggest whether Junia was a woman. They generally abound in reasons for their opinions.

But that *Junia* was a woman there is not the slightest reason to doubt.

(1.) We have four different editions of the Greek Testament, including the text from which the Revised version was made, and they all have Ι ο υ ν ιαν, Junia.

(2.) If in any of the manuscripts this word was written with the circumflex accent, showing that it might be a contraction, some of the sharp-eyed critics would have noticed it.

(3.) Chrysostom asserts positively that *Junia* was a woman.

2. Dr. Clarke expresses a doubt whether Junia was an apostle. He says: "*of note among the apostles.*" Whether this intimates that they were *noted apostles* or only highly respected *by the apostles*, is not absolutely clear; but the latter appears to me the most probable.

"They were not only well known to St. Paul, but also to the rest of the apostles."

Considering the prejudices of the age in which he lived, this doubt is a great concession.

But that Junia *was an apostle* will be evident to all

who will carefully weigh the following reasons:

1. Dean Alford says: "Two renderings are given: (1.) '*of note among the apostles!* so that *they themselves are counted among* the apostles; thus the Greek ff. In support of this view he refers to Chrysostom, Calvin, Est, Wolf, Tholuck, Kolln, Olshausen and others.

"Or (2.) '*noted among the apostles,' i.e. well known* and spoken of by the apostles. Thus Beza Grotius, Koppe, Reiche, Meyer, Fritz DeW. But, as Thol. remarks, had this latter been the meaning, we should have expected some expression like δ ι'απασων Των εκκλησιων. 2 Cor. 8:18, *throughout all the churches.*

"I may besides remark, that for Paul to speak of any persons *as celebrated among the apostles,* in sense (2), would imply that he had more frequent intercourse with the other apostles than we know that he had; and would besides be improbable on any supposition. The whole question seems to have sprung up in modern times from the idea that οι απστολοι must mean *the Twelve only.* If the wider sense found in Acts 14:4, 14. 2 Cor. 8:23. 1 Thess 2:6 (compare i:1) be taken, there need be no doubt concerning the meaning."

Dean Alford, then, has no doubt that Junia was an apostle.

Luther, in his German Bible, translates this clause as follows: "welche sind beruhmte Apostele." *who are renowned apostles.*

Chrysostom also makes the meaning clear beyond the shadow of a doubt. He was a man of great learning; the Greek was his native language; he was born A. D. 347, at Antioch. In his comments on this verse he says:

"*Who are of note among the apostles.* And indeed to be apostles at all is a great thing. But to be even amongst these of note, just consider what a great encomium this is! But they were of note owing to their works, to their achievements. Oh! how great is the devotion of this woman, that she should be counted worthy of the appellation of apostle! But even here he does not stop, but adds another encomium besides, and says, who were also in Christ before me."

Thus, Chrysostom plainly declares, 1. That Junia was a woman. 2. That she was an apostle.

Olshausen, in his comment on Rom. 16:7, says: "Junia appears to have been the wife of Andronicus.

"The title of apostle is of course to be taken here in the wider sense of the word." By "wider" he means not con-fined to the Twelve.

It is without dispute that the apostles are the highest order of the ministry. God has placed them in the highest rank.

Nowhere is it said in the New Testament that this order of the ministry became extinct with the first generation of Christians. God *has set* them in His church. No matter what arrangements men make, God raises up *apostles* from time to time. LUTHER was an *apostle,* sent by God to lead on the great Reformation.

JOHN WESLEY was an apostle.

ELIZABETH FRY was an apostle, sent by God to offer salvation to the hardest criminals; and to set in motion reformatory influences that will never cease to operate.

WILLIAM TAYLOR is as truly an apostle as St. Paul was.

Since, then, we find that, at the very beginning of the Christian church, a woman was an apostle, we should not, on account of her sex, exclude woman from any position in the church to which God may call her, and for which she possesses, in the judgment of those whose duty it is to decide in such matters, as ample qualifications as are required of men who aspire to the same position.

It is high time that the tyranny of sex was overthrown. And the Church of Jesus Christ should lead the way in treating all human beings with absolute impartiality.

Paul says he was ordained both a preacher and an apostle. – 1 Tim. 2:7; and so we may conclude that Junia was ordained.

God only can make apostles. But if he sends a woman out to do the work of an apostle, and she does it faithfully, why should we hesitate to give the Scriptural name to the office, to fill which she is called and qualified of God?

"What could I other than I did?
Could I a singing bird forbid?
Deny the wind stirred leaf? Rebuke
The music of the forest brook?"

— Whittier.

God gives lights that they may shine; and the church should cease its efforts to put out these lights, or to so wall them in as to limit to a small number those whom they may enlighten.

CHAPTER IX.

WOMEN PROPHETS.

"Thyself and thy belongings
Are not thine own so proper, as to waste
Thyself upon thy virtues, they on thee.
Heaven doth with us as we with torches do,
Not light them for themselves; for if our virtues
Did not go forth of us, 'twere all alike
As if we had them not."

– Shakespeare.

THAT women are to take a prominent part in evangelizing the world was as clearly foretold in the prophecies of old as was the Gospel itself. The first great prophecy declares that the seed of the woman "shall bruise the serpent's head." – Gen. 3:15. As Henry Melville says, "This is a wonderful passage, spreading itself over the whole of time, and giving outlines of the history of this world from the beginning to the final consummation." It was by "the seed of the woman," Christ, that our redemption was purchased.

Not only this, but it was predicted that woman was to have a distinguished part in making the glad tidings of salvation known. "The Lord gave the word, great was the company of those that published it." – Ps. 68:11.

As these words stand, in our common version, there does not appear in them anything out of the common order. It is quite otherwise in the original.

In his comment on this verse, Dr. Adam Clarke says: "*Of the female preachers there was a great host.* Such is the literal translation of this passage; the reader may make of it what he pleases."

We make of it a prediction that in the days spoken of in this psalm, when "Ethiopia shall stretch out her hands unto
God," women were to preach the Gospel.

In the Revised version a similar meaning to Dr. Clarke's translations is given –

"The Lord giveth the word;
The women that publish the tidings are a great host."

Bishop Horne regards this Psalm as one relating to the Messiah. He says: "It seems evidently to have been composed on that festive and joyful occasion, the removal of the ark to Mount Sion. Under this figure, David, foreseeing the exaltation of Messiah, speaks of him whom he describes as arising and vanquishing his enemies, as causing the faithful to rejoice, and showing mercy to the afflicted; as bringing his church out of bondage, supporting herein the world by the Word and the Spirit, purging away her corruptions, and subduing her adversaries."

In harmony with this, is the prophecy of Joel as quoted by St. Peter.

"And it shall come to pass in the last days, saith God, I will pour out of my Spirit upon all flesh; and your sons and your daughters shall prophesy, and your young men shall see visions, and your old men shall dream dreams; and on my servants and on my handmaidens I will pour out in those days of my Spirit and they shall prophesy." – Acts 2:18.

1. All the preaching here foretold is included in the word "prophesy."

2. No distinction whatever is made between the "sons and daughters," between the "servants and handmaidens." Whatever is affirmed of the one is affirmed of the other. No higher ministry is given to the sons than is given to the daughters. If one may be ordained so may the other.

This prediction was not exhausted on the day of Pentecost. It was to continue to be fulfilled throughout the entire Christian dispensation. This is implied in the words, *in the last days.* If on the day of Pentecost they were in "the last days," then certainly we are now in "the last days." Then are we to look for the same out-pouring of the Spirit on the women as on the men. Then have they the same divine right to declare, under the influence of the Holy Spirit, the wonderful power and great willingness of Christ to save.

Under the Old Dispensation, as we have seen, women were prophets.

At the coming of Christ, Anna was a prophetess. – Luke 2:36.

But these were the exceptions. Under the Gospel, the *rule* is that upon women, equally as upon men, the prophetic influence is to be poured out, and they are to prophesy. No distinction of sex is to be ob-served in the power and liberty given by God to speak for Him.

It must be kept in mind that the primary meaning of prophesy is to speak for another, to speak under the direct influence of the Spirit of God.

The first place in the Bible where the word prophet occurs is where God says of Abraham: *For he is a prophet, and he shall pray for thee.* – Gen. 20:7. Here is no allusion to the foretelling of future events. Dr. Adam Clarke says: "The proper ideal meaning of the original word is, *pray, entreat, make supplication.* Thus it is said that the *Spirit of God* came upon Saul and *he prophesied."* – 1 Sam. 10:10. But there is no intimation that he foretold future events.

But as God specially makes known His will to those who live in intimate communion with Him by prayer and faith, some of these men were inspired to foretell future events. Hence a prophet is generally considered to be one who foretells. But in the Bible sense, a prophet is one who speaks the truth of God, inspired by His spirit, whether this truth relates to things present or to come. A large part of the writings of the prophets recorded in the Old Testament are exhortations.

St. Paul declares: *But he that prophesieth speaketh*

unto men to edification and exhortation and comfort. – 1
Cor. 14:3. In his comment on this verse, Dr. Clarke
quotes Whitby: "The person who has the gift of *teaching* is much more useful to the church than he who
has only the gift of *tongues,* because he speaks to the
profit of men – viz: to their edification, by the Scriptures which he expounds; to their *exhortation* by what
he teaches; and to their comfort by his revelation."

Again, *Greater is he that prophesieth.* Says Dr.
Clarke: "A useful, zealous preacher, though unskilled
in learned languages, is much *greater* in the sight of
God, and in the eye of sound common sense, than he
who has the gift of those learned tongues; except he
interpret; and we seldom find *great scholars good
preachers.* This should humble the scholar who is too
apt to be proud of his attainments, and despise his
less learned, but more useful brother. This judgment
of St. Paul is too little regarded."

We come then to these

CONCLUSIONS.

1. That prophets are an established order of ministers in the Church of Christ. It was foretold in the
Old Testament, and declared in the New Testament,
that they should be.

2. That they rank next to the Apostles. *And God
hath set some in the church, first apostles, secondarily
prophets.* – 1 Cor. 12:28. See also Eph. 4:11, 12. This last
passage declares that God gives them *for the work of
the ministry, for the edifying of the body of Christ,* that is
for the sanctification of believers and the conversion
of sinners.

3. That in the New Testament sense, *prophets* are
those called of God, and inspired by His Spirit to
preach the Gospel.

4. That in the prophetic office not the slightest
distinction is made between women and men.

5. The inference is unavoidable that if men who
give satisfactory evidence to the church that they are
called of God to *prophesy,* that is, to *preach* should be
ordained, then women who give equally satisfactory

evidence that they are called of God to preach should be ordained. We see not how this conclusion can be avoided.

If it is evident that God has called a woman to his great work, and eminently adorned her with gifts and graces for its performance, then should the church speed her on her mission by solemnly endorsing it before the world, in setting her apart for the work to which God has called her. Whether done by man or woman, it is a work worthy of all recognition,

> "To guide the people in the way of truth
> By saving doctrine, and from error lead,
> To know, and knowing, worship God aright."

CHAPTER X.

DEACONS.

"Not unto manhood's heart alone
   The holy influence steals;
Warm with a rapture not its own,
   The heart of WOMAN feels.
As she who by Samaria's well
   The Saviour's errand sought –
As those who with the fervent Paul
   And meek Aquila wrought."

– Whittler.

IT is generally assumed that the seven, whose appointment as assistants of the Apostles is described in Acts 6:1-6, were deacons. Probably they were. We will not question it. But the fact deserves notice that they are never called deacons. It should also be borne in mind that the only record we have of their acts is of their performing the work of a preacher of the Gospel. "And Stephen, full of faith and power, did great wonders and miracles among the people." – Acts 6:8.

"And they were not able to resist the wisdom and the spirit by which he spake."

"It is said that Phillip, the evangelist, was one of the seven." – Acts 21:8. So that while "the seven" were to look after the charitable distributions of the church it nowhere appears that their work was confined to this. They were assistants of the Apostles, and as such they preached.

Nothing can be clearer than that the New Testament deacons were preachers.

"Who then is Paul, and who is Apollos, but

ministers,"(in the original deacons,) "by whom ye believed." – 1 Cor. 3:5.

"Who also hath made us able ministers (deacons), of the New Testament." – 2 Cor. 3:6.

"Whereof I was made a minister (deacon)." – Eph. 3:7.

"To all the saints in Christ Jesus which are at Philippi, with the bishops and deacons." – Phil. 1:1. Here the Apostle mentions but two classes or orders of ministers, one of which is the *deacons.*

"Whereof I, Paul, am made a minister (deacon). – Col. 1:23.

"Timotheus, our brother and *minister (deacon)* of God." – 1 Thess. 3:2.

In short, there is not *single passage* in which the word *deacon* is used to designate an *officer of the church*, where there is any indication that this deacon *was not a preacher.* But in the passages quoted above, and in other passages, there can be no doubt but that the person styled a *deacon* was a preacher. Then the conclusion must be that the New Testament deacons were preachers. They were all preachers.

Mosheim, in writing of the church in the first century, says: "Both presbyters and deacons preached and administered the sacrament of baptism, and the former the Lord's Supper."[22]

There are some passages in which the word is taken in its primary signification of *servant*, such as Mat. 23:11, John 2:5, 9, but in these passages the meaning is clear. They afford no more reason for asserting that the deacons of the church were servants, or any particular deacon was a *servant*, in the sense in which the word *servant* is commonly understood, than the use of the word *ecclesia* in Acts 19:39, proves that the same word in Rev. 2:1, shows that the "church of Ephesus" was not a church at all, but a riotous assembly.

When any words are given an ecclesiastical meaning in the New Testament they must always be understood as having that meaning when used in treating of church officers, and the connection warrants it. The word δ ι α κ ο ν ο ς, *deacon,* where used in the New Testament as referring to an officer of the church, when translated at all, in both our common and revised versions is uniformly translated *minister,* except in one solitary instance. *That is where it refers to a woman.* I commend unto you Phebe, our sister, which is a servant (in the original δ ι α κ ο ν ο ς, *deacon*) of the church which is at Cenchrea. – Rom. 16:1.

Here you see the power of prejudice in even learned and pious men. Paul, when called a *deacon,* our translators call a *minister,* but: Phebe, when called a *deacon* they make a *servant.* That there might be no dispute about her sex Paul calls her, *our sister.*

That there might be no doubt about her ecclesiastical position he calls her *deacon* or *minister of the church at Cenchrea.* Nothing can be more clear; nothing can be more definite.

The churches of that day had no *servants,* in the ordinary sense of the word servant. The churches were poor. Their meetings were held in private houses. They had no church edifices.

Here, then, we have a record in the New Testament of one woman who was a *minister.*

The apostle states the qualifications which the women deacons must possess.

"Even so *must their* wives *be* grave, not slanderers, sober, faithful in all things." – 1 Tim. 3:11. We had read this passage hundreds of times without suspecting its meaning. Lately, in reading it in the original, its meaning struck us as if by revelation. The word translated *wives* should be *women. Their* before wives is not found in the original. So that what the apostle here writes, is not about the *wives of deacons,* but about *women deacons.*

Chrysostom says of this, the eleventh, verse: "Some have thought that this was said of women generally, but it is not so, for why should he introduce anything about women to interfere with his subject? He is speaking of those who hold the rank of Deaconesses.

"This must be understood, therefore, to relate to deaconesses. For that order is necessary and useful and honorable in the church. Observe how he requires the same virtue from the Deacons as from the Bishops, for though they were not of equal rank, they must equally be blameless; equally pure."

Dr. Adam Clarke, in his comment on this verse, says:

"I believe the apostle does not mean here the wives either of the *bishops* or *deacons* in particular, but the Christian *women* in general. The original is simply γυναικας ωσαυτως σεμνας – *gunaikas osautos semnas. Let the women likewise be grave.* Whatever is spoken here becomes women in general; but if the apostle had those termed *deaconesses* in his eye, which is quite possible, the words are peculiarly suitable to *them*. That there was such an *order* in the apostolic and primitive church, and that they were appointed to their office by the *imposition of hands,* has already been noticed on Rom. 16:1. Possibly, therefore, the apostle may have had this *order of deaconesses* in view, to whom it was as necessary to give counsels and cautions as to the *deacons* themselves; and to prescribe their qualifications, lest improper persons should insinuate themselves into that office."

Considering the time when Dr. Clarke wrote, this was saying a great deal.

Dean Alford, one of the most learned of modern commentators, is still more explicit. In his Greek Testament, on this passage he says: "(The) women in like manner. Who are these? Are they (1) women who were to serve as deacons, – deaconesses? – or (2) wives of the deacons? – or (3) wives of the deacons and overseers? – or (4) women in general? I conceive we may dismiss (4) at once, for Chrysostom's reason.

'For why should he wish to insert anything about women foreign to the subject of which he was speaking?'

(3) Upheld by Calv. Est. Calev. and Mack, may for the same reason, seeing that he returns to διακονοι,

diakonoi, again in verse 12, be characterized as extremely improbable. (2) has found many supporters among modern commentators; Ludi, Beza. Beng., (who strangely adds, 'pendet ab *habentes,* ver. 9,) Rosenm. Heinr, Comyb., al., and E.V. But it has against it (*a*) the omission of all expressed reference to the deacons, such as might be given by αυτων, *auton their,* or by τἁς *tas, they;* (*b*) the expression of ωσαυτως, (osautos, likewise,) by which the διακονοι (deacons) themselves were introduced, and seems to mark a new ecclesiastical class; (*c*) the introduction of the injunction respecting the deacons, εστωσαν μιας γυναικος ανδρες (husbands of one wife) as a new particular, which would hardly be if their wives had been mentioned before; (*d*) the circumstances connected with the mention of Phebe as διακονος (deacon) of the church at Cenchrea on Rom. 16:1, that unless these are deaconesses, there would be among these injunctions no mention of an important class of persons employed as officers of the church.

We come thus to consider (1) that these γυναικες are *deaconesses,* ministrae, *ministers,* as Pliny calls them in his letter to Trajan. In this view the ancients are, as far as I know, unanimous. Of the moderns, it is held by Grot. Marb. Micb. DeW., Wiesinger, Ellicott. It is alleged against it – (*a*) that thus the return to the διακονοι, (deacons), ver. 12, would be harsh, or as Conyb. "on that view, the verse is most unnaturally interpolated in the midst of the discussion concerning the deacons."

But the ready answer to this is found in Chry's. view of ver 12, that under διακονοι, and their household duties he comprehends in fact both sexes under one; ταῦτα καὶ πετι γυναικῶυ διακόνων ἁρμόττει εἰρῆσϑαι – ("it is fitting that these things should be said about women deacons;") (*b*) that the existence of deaconesses as an order in the ministry is not after all so clear. To this it might be answered, that even were they nowhere else mentioned, the present passage stands on its own grounds; and if it seemed from the context that such persons were indicated here, we should reason from this to the fact of their existence, not from the absence of other mention to their non-indication here.

"I decide, therefore, (1) that these women are 'deaconesses; (must be), grave, not slanderers," corresponds to Μν δ ι λ ο γ ο υ ς (not double-tongued) in the males, being the vice to which the female sex is addicted; δ ι α β ο λ ο ς ("diabolos") in this sense (reff) is peculiar in N.T. to these epistles; "sober" corresponding to Μη ο ι ν ω π ο λ λ ω π ρ ο σ ε ρ χ ο ν τ α ς – (not given to much wine) "faithful in all things corresponds to Μη α ι σ χ ρ ο κ ε δ ε ι ς (not greedy of gain;) trusting in the distribution of the alms committed to them, and in all other ministrations.

12. General directions respecting those in the diaconate (of both sexes, the female being included in the male, see Chrys. cited above with regard to their domestic condition and duties, as above (verses 4, 5), respecting the episcopate."

We have given this learned note in full that none might think they are reading only a garbled extract. The careful English reader will have no difficulty in understanding it with the translations we have given.

Notice 1. That though he gives the strongest authorities to be found against his opinion, yet he himself is not in doubt as to the true meaning of the verse in question – 1 Tim. 3:11.

2. "I decide." What does he decide? That the apostle refers in this verse, not to women in general, nor to the wives of deacons, but to "women deacons, deaconesses." This is the conclusion of Dean Alford of the church of England, one of the most learned and honored of English prelates. With this view the most learned of modern commentators agree.

Olshausen's Commentary, edited by Prof. Kendrick, says on 1 Tim. 3:11: "It will scarcely admit of a doubt that γ υ ν α ι κ ε ς (gunaikes) here is to be understood as deaconesses. The apostle having specified the moral qualifications of a deacon, is led by the

71

homogeneousness of the office to connect with those such as are proper to deaconesses."

The American Commentary, edited by Alvah Hovey, D. D. LL. D., has the following on this verse: "Women in like manner – that is women filling the deacon's office, deaconesses." After giving contrary opinions, he says: "Decisive reasons, however, seem here to require its reference to the deaconesses, who may, indeed, often have been the wives of deacons, but who are here mentioned as the female members of the diaconate."

Jamieson, Faussett and Brown, in their comment on this verse, say:

"THEIR WIVES," rather "the women," *i.e.,* "the deaconesses." For there is no reason that special rules should be laid down as to the wives of the deacons, and not also as to the wives of the Bishops or overseers. Moreover, if the wives of the deacons were meant, there seems no reason for the omission of "their" (not in the Greek.) Also the Greek for "even so," (the same as for "likewise," v. 8, and "in like manner," ch. 2:9,) denotes a transition to another class of persons.

"Further, there were doubtless deaconesses, at Ephesus, such as Pheoebe was at Cenchrea (Rom. 16:1, "servant," Greek, "deaconess"), yet no mention is made of them in this epistle if not here; whereas, supposing them to be meant here, ch. 3, embraces in due proportion all the persons in the service of the church. Naturally, after specifying the qualifications of the deacons, Paul passes to those of the kindred office, the deaconess. "Grave" occurs in the case of both.

"Not slanderers" here, answers to "not double-tongued" in the deacons; so "not false accusers." (Titus 2:3.)

"Sober" here answers to "not given to much wine" in the case of the deacons, (v. 8). Thus it appears he requires the same qualifications in female deacons as in deacons, only with such modifications as the difference of sex suggested. Pliny, in his celebrated letters to

Trajan, calls them "female ministers." FAITHFUL IN
ALL THINGS – of life as well as faith. Trustworthy in
respect to the alms committed to them, and their other
functions, answering to "not greedy of filthy lucre,"
v. 8, in the case of the deacons."

Thus we see, 1. That the officers of the New Testament church called *deacons* were preachers of the
Gospel. They did other things, but these were inci-
dental to the preaching. They were a regularly constituted and acknowledged order of the ministry. Paul
addresses one of his epistles, "to all the saints in
Christ Jesus which are at Philippi, with the bishops
and deacons." The deacons were not laymen, but one
order of the ministry.

2. That in the New Testament church some of the
deacons were women.

3. That provision was made for women to be deacons in the church of Christ for all time to come, for the
qualifications that they must possess are given, as well
as the qualifications of the men who are deacons, and
these qualifications are essentially the same.

Then the New Testament gives to the Church
ample authority to ordain women for the work of the
ministry.

CHAPTER XI.

DEACONESSES.

"The breach though small at first, soon opening wide,
In rushes folly with a full-moon tide,
Then welcome errors of whatever size,
To justify it by a thousand lies.
As creeping ivy clings to wood or stone,
And hides the ruin that it feeds upon;
So sophistry cleaves close to and protects
Sin's rotten trunk, concealing its defects."

– Cowper.

THE deacons of the New Testament, as we have seen, were preachers. They were assistants of the apostles. They aided them in spreading a knowledge of the Gospel; for they were to *hold the mystery of the faith in a pure conscience.* – 1 Tim. 3:9. They attended to the distribution of the charities of the church, and assisted in administering the sacraments.

There is not, in the New Testament, the slightest intimation that the work of the deaconesses was, *in any respect, different from that of the deacons.*

The office was one – the functions the same.

A postmistress discharges all the duties, and enjoys all of the privileges of a postmaster.

A Queen, who succeeds to the throne in her own right, possesses all the prerogatives of a King. Elizabeth of England was no less a sovereign than her father, Henry VIII, whom she succeeded.

So a deaconess in the New Testament sense of the term, is simply a woman who possesses the functions and discharges the duties of a deacon.

Mosheim, in speaking of the Church of the first century, says: "The church had ever belonging to it, even from its very first rise, a class of ministers, composed of persons of either sex and who were termed deacons and deaconesses. Their office was to distribute the alms to the necessitous; to carry the orders or messages of the elders wherever necessary; and to perform various other duties, some of which related merely to the solemn assemblies that were held at stated intervals, whilst others were of a general nature."[23]

This opinion that the deacons and deaconesses were essentially the same, and were "a class of ministers," is doubtless correct. Their duties in the "solemn assemblies" were, in the absence of an elder, to conduct the services and preach the word.

"Learned men," says the same historian, "have been led to conclude, and apparently with much reason, that those who had given unequivocal proof of their faith and probity in the capacity of deacons, were, after a while elected into the order of presbyters."[24]

The practice of some of our modern churches of placing *deacons* where they belong, as *an order in the ministry*, eligible to promotion, and classing *deaconesses* among *lay-workers*, without any possibility of ever rising to the higher ministries of the church, has neither reason nor Scripture for its support. It is giving a stone to those who call for bread. It is conferring a shadow and withholding the substance; it is bestowing a name and keeping back that which is implied in the name. In short it is a stupendous sham, of which any body of men claiming common honesty should be ashamed. It is an insult to womankind, and should be resented by them as such. Every woman should refuse to accept the name unless there is given with it all that is implied in the name.

It is a wonderful presumption upon the ignorance or servility of its members, for a great church to say in its book of discipline: "The duty of a Traveling

Deacon is:

1. To administer Baptism and to solemnize Matrimony.

2. To assist the Elder in administering the Lord's Supper.

3. To do all the duties of a Traveling Preacher."

"The duties of the deaconesses are to minister to the poor, visit the sick, pray with the dying, care for the orphan, seek the wandering, comfort the sorrowing, save the sinning, and, relinquishing wholly all other pursuits, devote themselves, in a general way, to such forms of Christian labor as may be suited to their abilities."

All these things may be good and important. That is not the question. But why make the duties of Deacons and Deaconesses so widely different? Why clothe the men deacons with ministerial dignity, and send them into the pulpit to preach, and into the altar to help administer the sacraments; and refuse these prerogatives to the *women deacons*, but send them to the garrets and cellars to hunt up the depraved, the destitute and the dying? Why give to the deacons the dignity and to the deaconesses the drudgery? What reason or Scripture is there for such partiality? The State does not make such odious distinctions. When Maria Theresa fell heir to the throne of Austria and Hungary, though the laws of Hungary recognized males only as successors to the Kingly power, she presented herself before her nobles with her babe in her arms, and the nobles, with one voice, shouted, "Hungarians, behold your *King!*" Not a monarch of her day had a more loyal following, or a more vigorous and glorious reign. Though a Queen she had all the prerogatives of a King.

What would be thought of a Board of Education that, in its proposals for Teachers should say:

"It shall be the duty of the School Master to instruct their pupils, maintain order and discharge the duties of a School Teacher.

"It shall be the duty of the School Mistress to look

up poor children, provide for them, bind up the wounds of those that get hurt, and devote her whole time to labors among necessitous children."

All this might be necessary and useful, but the number of qualified female teachers who would apply for the position would be small.

No. The disgraceful business of insulting womanhood, by giving to woman an office with an honorable name, and then divesting that office of the functions that belong to it when filled by a man, is confined to professed churches of Jesus Christ. Women ought to put an end to it by refusing to submit to such a glaring imposition.

To relieve the suffering is a Christlike work. In it all Christians and especially Christian ministers should bear a part. If the church depute it to some of its more devoted female members, we will not complain, but the church should not dignify these almoners of its bounty with a ministerial title, and yet forbid them to exercise the functions belonging to that order of the ministry, which bears the same title.

> "And the parson made it his text that
>   week and he said likewise,
> That a lie which is half a truth is ever
>   the blackest of lies,
> That a lie which is all a lie may be met
>   and fought with outright,
> But a lie which is part a truth is a
>   harder matter to fight."
>   – *Tennyson.*

That a Christian church may have women deacons is true; but this truth loses its essence by refusing to give to this office the functions that belong to it when filled by men.

CHAPTER XII.

EVANGELIZING THE WORLD.

"Lo! in the clouds of heaven appears
God's well-beloved Son;
He brings a train of brighter years,
His Kingdom is begun.
He comes a guilty world to bless
With mercy, truth and righteousness."

– Bryant.

THE progress of the Gospel is slow. A large part of the human race have never heard of Christ. The darkness of idolatry rests upon a great majority of the families of the Earth. The number of heathen and Mohammedans is vastly greater than the number of even nominal Christians.

In the most favored Christian lands, how few *real* Christians are found! How small the numbers who even profess to be born of God! and of these how small the proportion who give Scriptural evidence of this supernatural change! "We know that whosoever is born of God sinneth not; but he that is begotten of God keepeth himself, and that wicked one toucheth him not" – 1 Jno. 5:18.

"How monstrous," says Finney, "and how melancholy the fact, that the great mass of professing Christians to this day recognize the 7th and not the 8th chapter of Romans as their own experience! According to this, the new birth or regeneration does not break the power of the propensities over the will. The truth is, and must not be disguised, that they have not any just idea of regeneration. They mistake con-

viction for regeneration. They are so enlightened as to
perceive and affirm their obligation to deny the flesh,
and often resolve to do it, but in fact do it not. They
only struggle with the flesh, but are continually wor-
sted and brought into bondage: and this they call a
regenerate state. O, sad! How many thousands of
souls have been blinded by this delusion and gone
down to hell!"

What is the cause of this comparative failure of
Christianity? The Gospel is designed by God for all
nations. It is adapted to them. It is intended for every
individual. It gives a happiness that nothing else can
afford. Every nation that embraces Christianity is
elevated by it. Prosperity attends its progress. In its
triumphal march it scatters blessings with a lavish
hand. Wherever it goes, it establishes schools and
churches, it builds homes and hospitals, it brings
peace and comfort. Yet this outward prosperity is but
"the dust of that diamond which constitutes her
crowning gift – the shed blossoms of that tree of life
of which the office of Christ is to dispense the immortal fruit." Even opposers of the Gospel admit the beneficent effects of the Gospel. "So conspicuous have
been the triumphs of the cross in many of the most
hopeless parts of the heathen world, that even the
magicians of worldly philosophy begin to acknowledge that this is the finger of God, and to despair of
ever being able to do the same with their enchant-
ments."

Why then is not the Gospel carried to the ends of
the earth? Why is it not preached to every creature? It
is not for lack of means. Money is poured out freely
for enterprises bearing the Christian name, but serv-
ing chiefly as monuments of pride. The amount ex-
pended to build and run a fashionable church would
build and run a dozen equally commodious, and better adapted to the spread of Christianity. But the Gospel does not depend on edifices; it can use money,
but it is not dependent upon it. The apostles went out
without purse or scrip. The early evangelists had no

salaries. One can be converted in a tent more easily than in a cathedral, as cathedrals are controlled. A multitude assembled under God's great canopy is as accessible to divine truth as if they were standing in Westminster Abbey. It was their out-door work which made Wesley and Whitfield the great apostles of their day.

Nor is it for lack of influence that the Gospel does not make more rapid progress in Christian and in heathen lands. Our great statesmen, and soldiers, and men of science openly avow their belief of the Gospel. Said Henry Clay: "I believe in the truth of Christianity, though I am not certain of having experienced that change of heart which divines call the new birth. But I trust in God, and Jesus, and I hope for immortality. I have tried the world and found its emptiness. It cannot fill and satisfy the human mind."

Says Stephens, a celebrated literary man of England: "In the long annals of skeptical philosophy no single name is to be found to which the gratitude of mankind has been yielded or is justly due." The benefactors of mankind are Christians. The Gospel is no longer an experiment. Its beneficent effects are seen and acknowledged. This of itself opens the way for the heralds of the cross.

In addition to all these human influences in its favor, the Gospel, wherever it is faithfully proclaimed, carries with it a divine energy that nothing but the free will of man can withstand. It is the "power of God unto salvation to every one that believeth." The promise, "Lo, I am with you alway, even unto the end of the world," still holds good. Where Christ is, there His power is exerted, silently it may be, but nevertheless powerfully for the good of all present. No other advocate has such assistance as he who, possessed of the Holy Spirit, advocates the Gospel. He may be wanting in human learning. Men may oppose him and persecute him, and put him to death, but they are not "able to withstand the wisdom and the Spirit by which he speaks." There is a convincing power in his plain, simple words to which it is difficult to reply.

Melancthon said: "That Luther's words were born, not on his lips, but in his soul."

Why, then, we repeat, does not Christianity root out all false religions? and why does it not have a more marked effect upon the lives of those who acknowledge its truth? There must be a cause.

The reason is, *that the vast majority of those who embrace the Gospel are not permitted to labor according to their ability, for the spread of the Gospel.*

It is said that about two-thirds of all the members of all the Protestant churches of this country are women. Yet in these churches a woman, no matter what may be her qualification, and devotion, and zeal, is not permitted to occupy the same position as a man. The superior must, sometimes, give place to the inferior. The bungler must give directions, the adept must obey. The incompetent coward must command, if no competent man is found, while the competent woman is relegated to the rear. A Deborah may arise, but the churches, by their laws, prohibit her from coming to the front. And these laws must be enforced though all others are disregarded.

In some of the churches a woman is forbidden to speak or pray in even a social meeting if men are present! In none of these, except among the Friends, is woman given the same position, or the same opportunity for advancement as the man. She is, of set purpose, kept back, while cunning contrivances are adopted to make her think that she is accorded all the liberty she wants. She suffers in consequence, but the cause of God suffers most.

What a loss the world would have sustained if John Wesley had been suppressed in infancy! The work which Frances Willard is doing in the cause of temperance, and of moral reform, gives us some idea of what woman is capable of doing when left free to exercise the gifts and graces which God has given her. It is impossible to estimate the extent to which

81

humanity has suffered by the unreasonable and unscriptural restrictions which have been put upon women in the churches of Jesus Christ. Had they been given, since the days of the first Apostles, the same rights as men, this would be quite another world. Not only would the Gospel have been more generally diffused among mankind, but its influence, where its truth is acknowledged, would have been inconceivably greater. Our so-called Christian nations would have been more in harmony with the teachings of Christ, in their laws, their institutions and their practices.

CHAPTER XIII.

REQUIRED.

"In God's own might
We gird us for the coming fight,
And strong in Him, whose cause is ours,
In conflict with unholy powers,
We grasp the weapons He has given,
The Light, and Truth, and Love of Heaven."

– Whittier.

"*WHY ordain* women as long as the right to preach is quite generally conceded to them? Why should they not be satisfied with the privileges they now enjoy?"

Reader, will you consider candidly our answers to these questions?

The last, great Command of Christ requires that they who make converts should be invested with authority to administer the sacrament of baptism. "Go ye, therefore, and teach all nations, baptizing them in the name of the Father, and of the Son, and of the Holy Ghost; teaching them to observe all things whatsoever I have commanded you, and, lo, I am with you alway, even unto the end of the world. Amen." – Mat. 28:19, 20.

Notice the close connection of *teach* and *baptize* in this important text: *Go ye, therefore, and make disciples of all the nations, baptizing them.* – R.V. This certainly implies that those who make disciples for Christ, – get sinners converted, should, as a rule, baptize them. The same persons who are commanded to make disciples are commanded to baptize them. Till they have

83

done this, their work is not complete. The one is a part of their mission as well as the other. They who catch the fish may string the fish.

These revivalists may be "proved first," (1 Tim. 3:10,) but if found worthy and reliable, they should be clothed with authority to administer the sacraments to those whom they get converted.

If a woman, then, is permitted to hold revivals, – to do the work of an evangelist, – she should, when properly tried, if found duly qualified, be ordained. The churches must either stop her work or allow her to complete her work. Woman must either be permitted to baptize, or she must not be permitted to make converts.

By the present arrangement, the Churches separate what God has joined together.

"Must, then, every one who gets a sinner converted, baptize him?"

We do not affirm this. But if he keeps on getting sinners converted, and is evidently called of God to make this the business of life, then the Church, when it is satisfied of this, should authorize him to administer the sacraments. Whoever makes full proof of a call to the ministry should, in due time, be invested with the full functions of the ministry.

In oriental countries, where women are kept in great seclusion, it is necessary that women should be authorized to administer baptism to their female converts. That this right is not conceded is one reason why the progress of the Gospel is comparatively so slow in those lands.

Miss Fannie J. Sparkes, a well-known, able missionary to India, sends us the following incident:

"I was in camp at Bahere, in the Bareilly district, with Rev. and Mrs. J. H. Gill. We went one evening to the house of a poor, low caste man in a near village where three men and one woman were to be baptized. A number of the neighbors came in; all sat on the ground in the little enclosed yard in front of the house, the men on one side and the women on the other. The baptismal service began, and when the usual questions were asked, simplified so as to be easily understood by the candidates, the men responded readily, but the woman remained silent. Mr. Gill tried to persuade her to respond, but in vain; and finally said to me, 'You ask her the questions.' I did so, and immediately received ready, satisfactory replies.

"The three men were then baptized; the woman was kneeling in the midst of a little group of women near Mrs. Gill and myself. As Mr. Gill was about to place his hand upon her head, with a quick, nervous movement she drew her chaddah over her face, and put her head upon the ground in a position quite out of the reach of his hand, and could not be induced to consent to the baptism that evening. We got her to promise to visit us at our tents the next morning, which she did, and after some persuasion, she again consented to be baptized. The questions were put and answered as before; the little woman was growing painfully nervous and began to give her chaddah little twitches, as the minister was again about to place his hand upon her head. Seeing that she was likely to repeat the action of the previous evening, I placed my hand upon her head. She recognized the touch and remained perfectly quiet until the ceremony was finished."

To this woman, as to every one of the millions of women of India, the touch of the hand of any man except that of her husband means pollution. It is the necessary result of the education of centuries. Do you say it is a prejudice? If so, it is one to be admired; and one which the Church of Christ should respect. It is impossible for a nation to become a Christian nation until its women become Christians. The women of India must be reached mainly by women. Then there should be women missionaries, clothed with authority to administer all the ordinances, as well as to offer all the consolations of the Christian religion.

But Christianity is intended for all lands. It is

adapted to all nations. The churches of America should adopt such regulations as will enable them to meet the wants of the people of Asia.

Again, it is unjust to invite a woman to become a worker in the Church, and then, whatever may be her qualifications, her abilities and her success, forever exclude her by arbitrary enactments from its higher ministries.

Honorable worldlings do not act so unjustly. Is a woman permitted to teach a primary class in our schools? Then may she, when qualified, teach Latin and Greek and Algebra, become Principal and even school Superintendent. The highest scholastic honors are not withheld from her simply because she is a woman. Dartmouth and Columbia, two of our renowned Colleges, conferred, each of them, the title of LL. D. on Maria Mitchell, one of the greatest astronomers of the age.

When the captain and owner of a Mississippi river boat suddenly died, his wife assumed command, and when the civil authorities, after a rigid examination, found that she possessed the necessary qualifications, they promptly licensed her as a Captain. Her sex did not debar her from promotion in a calling for which men are specially adapted. Nor was the precedent considered dangerous. The gallant sailors did not fear that they would be superseded by women as commanders of ships.

Is a woman permitted to conduct a trial in a Justice's Court? She may also be admitted to practice in the higher courts. There is, in the aggregate, quite a number of women lawyers in the several states. Yet the men of the world do not appear to have any apprehension lest they should be crowded out of the legal profession.

Woman owes her elevation to Christianity. She shows her appreciation by rallying around the cross of Christ.

Justice, then, demands that all barriers placed by men in the way of the elevation of woman to any office in the gift of the church be removed.

"Even if we could do without them," writes John Stuart Mill, "would it be consistent with justice to refuse to them their fair share of honor and distinction, or to deny to them the equal moral right of all human beings to choose their occupation (short of injury to others) according to their own preferences, at their own risk? Nor is the injustice confined to them; it is shared by those who are in a position to benefit by their services. To ordain that any kind of persons shall not be physicians, or shall not be advocates, or shall not be members of parliament, is to injure not them only, but all who employ physicians or advocates, or elect members of parliament, and who are deprived of the stimulating effect of greater competition on the exertions of the competitors, as well as restricted to a narrower range of individual choice."

CHAPTER XIV.

FITNESS.

"'Tis hers to pluck the amaranthine flower
Of Faith, and round the Sufferer's temples bind
Wreaths that endure affliction's heaviest shower,
And do not shrink from sorrow's keenest wind."
— *Wordsworth*

NATURALLY, woman is, to say the least, equally qualified with men for the ministry of the Gospel.

A celebrated skeptic bears the following testimony to the character of woman:

"I tell you women are more prudent than men. I tell you, as a rule, women are more truthful than men. I tell you that women are more faithful than men – ten times as faithful as men. I never saw a man pursue his wife into the very ditch and dust of degradation and take her in his arms. I never saw a man stand at the shore where she had been morally wrecked, waiting for the waves to bring back even her corpse to his arms; but I have seen woman do it. I have seen woman with her white arms lift man from the mire of degradation, and hold him to her bosom as though he were an angel."

Dr. Lardner says of the women of Jerusalem in the days of Christ: "The number of women who believed in Jesus as the Christ, and professed faith in Him was not inconsiderable. Many of these there were, who had so good understanding, and so much virtue, as to overcome the common and prevailing prejudice. Without any bias or passion or worldly interests, and contrary to the judgments and menaces

of men in power, they judged rightly in a contro-
verted point, of as much importance as was ever de-
bated on earth."[25]

A Greek writer of the second century said: "It is
wonderful what women these Christians have."

1. Women comprehend and drink in the Spirit of
the Gospel more readily than men.

Christ very plainly told the Twelve that he would
rise again the third day. But they did not seem to understand it. But the women appeared to understand
it; and, at early dawn, on the third morning "came
Mary Magdalene and the other Mary to see the sepul-
chre." They were on the lookout, and to them Christ
first showed himself after his resurrection. It was a
woman that he commissioned to go to his disciples
and foretell them of his ascension. Woman entered
readily into the spirit of his words. It was in the apostolic church that woman began to teach the teachers
of the Christian religion. Fettered as she has been,
Christianity owes much to her for the progress it has
already made.

Clovis, King of the Franks, was a great warrior,
and a pagan. His people, too, were idolaters. He married Clotilde, a Burgundian princess, a Christian, absorbed in works of piety and charity. Through her
influence he became a Christian. To Remi, a godly
bishop whom his wife had sent for, in about the year
A. D. 496, to baptize him, he said: "I will listen to
thee, most holy father, willingly; but there is a difficulty. The people that follow me will not give up
their gods." The King called the people together.
They were better disposed than he thought they
were. The influence of his wife had been more powerful than he supposed. The great multitude cried out:
"We abjure the mortal gods; we are ready to follow
the immortal God whom Remi preacheth." So France
became a Christian nation.

About the year A. D. 568, Ethelbert, King of Kent
in England, married Bertha, the only daughter of
Caribert, King of Paris, one of the descendants of

Clovis. Ethelbert and his Saxons were fierce warriors, and staunch idolaters. But his wife, devout, irreproachable in conduct, exerted her influence to the utmost, for the conversion of her husband, and the Anglo-Saxons with their King embraced Christianity.

If woman has done so much, under the restrictions placed upon her in the days of barbarism, under the reign of force, and which have been perpetuated to our day, what might she not have done had all restrictions on account of sex been removed, and she been free to exert her abilities to the utmost in the cause of Christ?

Fenelon was one of the most godly, learned and useful ministers that has ever taught in the Roman Catholic church. But he was free to acknowledge that he received spiritual instruction from Madame Guion. His writings on religious experience are read with deep interest by Protestants to this day.

The work begun by John Wesley was carried on mainly by uneducated preachers. But for his employment of these lay-preachers, there is no reason to believe that the work of Wesley would have had any greater permanence than did that of Whitefield. But for the adoption of this powerful agency Wesley was indebted to his mother.

Mr. Wesley was a strong churchman, and could not tolerate any violation of what he considered the order of the Church. Thomas Maxfield was the first layman among his followers who attempted to preach.

"It was," says Dr. Adam Clarke, "in Mr. Wesley's absence that Mr. Maxfield began to preach. Being informed of this new and extraordinary thing, he hastened back to London to put a stop to it. Before he took any decisive step, he spoke to his mother on the subject, and informed her of his intention. She said, (I have had the account from Mr. Wesley himself):

"My son, I charge you before God, beware what you do: for Thomas Maxfield is as much called to preach the Gospel as you were.' This was one of the last things that a person for such high church principles might be expected to accede to."[26]

But in this, as in many other things, Mr. Wesley followed the advice of his mother. The survival of Methodism is largely, and I think wholly, due to this. If the work had been carried on only by the labors of clergymen of the Church of England, it never would have attained to the proportions it did; and it would have been absorbed by the Church.

If, then, women are quicker than men to comprehend the mystery of godliness, if they have keener spiritual perceptions, and deeper intuitions, they should not be, by arbitrary enactments, excluded on account of their sex, from any position that can make their influence more widely felt. Every one should be placed in the position where she can do most good.

2. *Woman has a special aptitude for teaching.*

This is acknowledged by the general selection of women to teach in our public schools. They succeed as teachers.

In the work of the ministry, so far as they have been permitted to attempt it, women have acquitted themselves as creditably as men.

Where they have labored, prejudices have been removed.

His biographer says that Adam Clarke had "considerable prejudice against this kind of ministry." But he went to a circuit on which *Miss Mary Sewel* had preached.

"Meeting her, he questioned her concerning her call. She modestly answered, by referring him to the places where she had preached, and wished him to inquire whether any good had been done. He did so, and heard of numbers who had been awakened under her ministry, and with several of them he conversed, and found their experience in Divine things Scriptural and solid. He thought, then, This is God's work, and if he chooses to convert men by employing such means, who am I that I should criticise the ways of God?"

After hearing her preach he wrote: "I have this morning heard Miss Sewel preach; she has a good talent for exhortation, and her words spring from a heart that evidently feels deep concern for the souls of the people; and consequently her hearers are interested and affected. I have formerly been no friend to female preaching, but my sentiments are a little altered. If God give to a holy woman a gift for exhortation and reproof, I see no reason why it should not be used. This woman's preaching has done much good; and fruits of it may be found copiously in different places in the circuit. I can therefore adopt the saying of a shrewd man, who, having heard her preach, and being asked his opinion of the lawfulness of it, answered, 'An *ass* reproved Balaam, and a cock reproved Peter, and why may not a *woman* reprove sin?'

"Such women should be patterns of all piety, of unblamable conversation, correct and useful in their *families*, and furnished to every good work. This certainly is the character of Miss Sewel, and may she ever maintain it."

Hearing another woman preacher, Mrs. Proudfoot, he wrote: "She spoke several pertinent things, which tended both to conviction and consolation; and seems to possess genuine piety. If the Lord choose to work in this way, shall my eye be evil because he is good? God forbid! Rather let me extol the God who, by contemptible instruments and the foolishness of preaching, saves those who believe in Jesus. Thou, Lord, choosest to confound the wisdom of the world by *foolishness*, and its *strength* by *weakness*, that no soul may glory in thy presence, and the excellency of the power may be seen to belong to thee alone. Had not this been the case, surely I had never been raised up to call sinners to repentance."

This testimony is the more valuable, coming from a reluctant witness, who confesses that he was prejudiced.

To the objection that such cases are exceptions, we reply in the words of John Stuart Mill:

"It is not sufficient to maintain that women on the average are less gifted than men on the average, with certain of the higher mental faculties, or that a smaller number of women than of men are fit for occupations and functions of the highest intellectual character. It is necessary to maintain that no women at all are fit for them, and that the most eminent women are inferior in mental faculties to the most mediocre of the men on whom those functions at present devolve. For if the performance of the function is decided either by competition, or by any mode of choice which secures regard to the public interest, there needs be no apprehension that any important employments will fall into the hands of women inferior to the average men, or to the average of their male competitors. The only result would be that there would be fewer women than men in such employments; a result certain to happen in any case, if only from the preference always likely to be felt by the majority of women for the one vocation in which there is nobody to compete with them. Now, the most determined depreciator of women will not venture to deny, that when we add the experience of recent times to that of ages past, women, and not a few, merely, but many women, have proved themselves capable of everything, perhaps without a single exception, which is done by men, and of doing it successfully and creditably. The utmost that can be said is, that there are many things which none of them have succeeded in doing as well as they have been done by some men – many in which they have not reached the very highest rank. But there are extremely few, dependent on mental faculties, in which they have not attained the rank next the highest. Is not this enough, and much more than enough, to make it a tyranny to them, and a detriment to society, that they should not be allowed to compete with men for the exercise of these functions? Is it not a mere truism to say, that such functions are often filled by men far less fit for them than numbers of women, and who would be beaten by women in any fair field of competition?"

3. The practical turn of woman's mind specially fits her for the work of the Gospel ministry.

Women generally are not given to abstractions. They make the most of the realities about them. Cases occur where the father of a family, overwhelmed with misfortune, dies in despair; the mother, though unused to the management of affairs, gathers up the fragments, gradually retrieves their fortunes, and raises her family in respectability and honor.

In the year 1348 a fearful plague, which started in China, visited Europe. In London, one hundred thousand people died. Italy lost half its inhabitants. It is estimated that in Europe twenty five million people perished. The survivors were panic-stricken. Men tried to stop the plague by murdering the Jews. In Mayence alone, twelve thousand of this persecuted race were sacrificed in the vain hope of stopping the ravages of this terrible plague.

Then they tried a painful, humiliating penance. They formed companies, called Flagellants, and marched from town to town in procession, robed in sombre garments, with red crosses on their breasts, their faces bent down, and bearing in their hands triple scourges having points of iron, with which, at stated times, they lacerated their bodies till the blood ran down to the ground.

The women, more sensible, formed bands to nurse and tend the sick. The miseries they could not prevent they sought to alleviate.

This disposition of woman to look at the present, and make the best of existing circumstances, would be of great benefit to the cause of Christianity if all restrictions on account of sex were removed, and she were left free to do good according to her inclination and ability.

4. Women are not wanting in the courage and

fortitude essential to the minister of the Gospel. The
bold Peter denied Christ, but the New Testament
gives us no account of any woman who opened her
mouth against him in the face of danger. The annals
of the church, in the days of persecution, tell us of
many a noble, tender, gentle woman who met death
in its most terrific form rather than deny Christ.

At Port Royal, in the days of Louis XIV., were
assembled some women of noble birth and great talents, who had consecrated themselves wholly to God,
and who made it their one business to serve and
please Him in all things. Though devout Catholics,
the doctrine of holiness which they taught rendered
them obnoxious to worldly ecclesiastics and a corrupt
court. The Archbishop of Paris made them a visit to
persuade them to renounce their faith. Not succeed-
ing, he said angrily as he left:

"They are pure as angels and proud as demons."

Persecution was kindled against them. To a friend
who came to see her, Mother Angelica said:

"Madame, when there is no God I shall lose courage; but so long as God is God, I shall hope in Him."

Jacqueline Pascal wrote: "What have we to fear?
Banishment and dispersion for the nuns, seizure of
temporalities, imprisonment and death, if you will;
but is not that our glory, and should it not be our joy?
Let us renounce the Gospel or follow the maxims of
the Gospel, and deem ourselves happy to suffer
somewhat for righteousness' sake. I know that it is
not for daughters to defend the truth, though one
might say, unfortunately, that since the bishops have
the courage of daughters, the daughters must have
the courage of bishops: but, if it is not for us to defend the truth, it is for us to die for the truth, and suffer everything rather than abandon it."

Of woman's mental ability to meet all the require-
ments of the Christian ministry, but little more need
be said. It is not long, since colleges were closed
against women, because they were not thought capable of acquiring a complete and thorough educa-

tion. But experience has demonstrated that there are women capable of standing side by side with men in the highest departments of scholarship.

The higher mathematics are generally considered the severest test of intellectual strength. Yet several women have excelled as mathematicians. Caroline Herschel, who died in 1848, aged 98 years, was one of the great astronomers of the world. She was elected a member of the Royal Society, which conferred on her their gold medal for completing the catalogue of nebulae and stars observed by her brother. One of her astronomical works was published at the expense of the Royal Society.

In the colleges to which young women are admitted, they at least come up to the average standing of young men.

If, then, woman has the spiritual discernment, the aptitude for teaching, the prudence and courage necessary to qualify her for the work of the ministry in all its departments, why not ordain her? Why deprive the church and the world, in any degree, of the services they need, and which she is able and willing to render?

CHAPTER XV.

GOVERNING.

> "Mightier far
> Than strength of nerve, or sinew, or the sway
> Of magic potent over sun and star,
> Is love, though oft to agony distrest,
> And though his favorite seat be feeble woman's breast."
> — *Wordsworth.*

"*IF* women are ordained, it will open the way for them to take a prominent part in the Government of the Church."

And why should they not? "Because Paul says: "I suffer not a woman to usurp authority over the man." – 1 Tim. 2:12.

But to exercise authority with which one is *lawfully invested,* is not to *usurp* authority. Queen Victoria exercises authority over men; but she is not a usurper.

Dean Alford translates this passage, *nor to lord it over.*

In the original, the word is αὐθεντειν, authentein, *to be a despot.* Neither must *men be lords over God's heritage.* – 1 Pet. 5:3.

Women took a prominent part in the government of the apostolic church.

The apostles, inspired as they were, did not assume to govern the Church. They recognized the authority to govern as belonging *to the church itself – to the men and women* of whom it was composed.

The first Christian church met in Jerusalem, in an upper room. *The women* are specially mentioned as being present. – Acts 1:14. Peter stood up in the midst of the disciples, and addressed them: "Men and brethren." These words, like the word "disciples," are generic terms, and include both men and women. He told them that, out of the men who had companied with them from the beginning, "must one be ordained to be a witness with us of his resurrection." – Acts 1:22. *And they appointed two.* The word "they" here refers to the whole body of the disciples, of whom "there were together about one hundred and twenty." Thus the members of the Church, and not the apostles, made the selection.

Again, when the twelve needed assistants to minister to the necessities of dependent believers, they did not themselves make the selection. They called together *the multitude of the disciples.* That this *multitude* included women, there can be no question. To them the apostles said: "Wherefore, brethren, look ye out among you seven men of honest report, full of the Holy Ghost and wisdom, whom we may appoint over this business." – Acts 6:3. *"And this saying pleased the whole multitude."* They chose seven: "Whom they set before the apostles; and when they had prayed, they laid their hands on them." – Acts 6:6. The *whole* does not mean *a part* – much less the smaller part. He who asserts that women had no place in this transaction must furnish proof for the assertion. But none can be had. The *whole multitude* of the disciples comprehends women.

There is no Scripture which forbids the ordination of woman on the ground that, being ordained, she will have a part in the government of the church.

The *elders* were rulers, in both the Jewish and the Christian church. "Let the elders that rule well be counted worthy of double honor, especially they who labor in the word and doctrine." – 1 Tim. 5:17. The word "elder," in the original, as in the English, is in the comparative degree. It is found sixty-seven times in the New Testament. In sixty-three passages it evidently means a church officer. It is used in the following passages only, in its primary signification of *one older* than another. "Now his *elder* son was in the field." – Luke 15:22. "And your *old men* shall dream dreams." – Acts 2:17. "Likewise ye younger submit yourselves unto the *elder*." – 1 Pet. 5:5.

Concerning one passage is there a doubt. "Rebuke not an elder but entreat him as a father." – 1 Tim. 5:1. If, as the translators of both our common, and of the Revised, versions, appear to think, the word *elder* here denotes an officer of the church, then we contend the same meaning should be given it in the second verse, which is a part of the same sentence. Then it would read: "The women elders as mothers," instead of "the elder women."

No writer who aims at clearness would use, in the same connection, and in the same sentence, the word King in one sense, and the word Queen in another.

If the word elder is to be taken here, where it refers to men, as it is used generally in the New Testament, to denote an officer of the church, then must it have the same meaning in the same sentence where it refers to women.

We must not change the meaning of words, as is done when πρεσβυτερος, presbuteros, is translated "elder" in one clause of this verse, and the same word, in the feminine form, is translated "elder women" in another clause of the same sentence. This appears to be done in order to adjust this text to the theory, that women must not have the same part as men in the governing of the church.

That woman possesses the administrative ability to exercise properly all the governing power usually vested in ordained preachers of the Gospel, is fully demonstrated by experience. That some women can govern well, we know, because some women have governed well. It is not a matter of theory. It is a demonstrated fact. Occasionally a woman has been placed at the head of the government of a country. In all such cases her administration will compare favorably with that of the men who preceded and followed her. Queen Elizabeth's reign was not eclipsed by that of any monarch of her day. The historian Hume says of Elizabeth:

"Few sovereigns of England succeeded to the throne in more difficult circumstances, and none ever conducted the government with such uniform success and felicity.

"Her vigor, her constancy, her magnanimity, her penetration, vigilance, address, are allowed to merit the highest praises, and appear not to have been surpassed by any person that ever filled a throne.

"Though unacquainted with the practice of toleration, the true secret for managing religious factions, she preserved her people by her superior prudence, from those confusions in which theological controversy had involved all the neighboring nations; and though her enemies were the most powerful princes of Europe, the most active, the most enterprising, the least scrupulous, she was able by her vigor to make deep impressions on their states; her own greatness, meanwhile, remained untouched and unimpaired.

"The wise ministers and brave warriors who flourished under her reign, share the praise of her success; but instead of lessening the applause due to her, they make great addition to it. They owed, all of them, their advancement to her choice; they were supported by her constancy; and, with all their abilities, they were never able to acquire any undue ascendant over her. In her family, in her court, in her kingdom, she remained equally mistress."[27]

Catharine II. of Russia was one of the ablest monarchs of her day. She was a German princess by birth. Elizabeth, Empress of Russia, chose her to become the wife of her nephew Peter, heir to her throne. On seeing her betrothed, the princess was so disappointed that she became sick, and was confined to her bed for weeks. However, she resigned herself to her fate; and was married at the age of seventeen. She applied herself to study, and mastered the Russian language, became familiar with the customs of the people, and won their affections.

Elizabeth died January 5, 1762, and Peter III. as-

cended the throne of Russia. He banished his wife to
a separate abode, and abandoned himself to drunkenness and debauchery. At the instigation of his mistress he formed the design of divorcing his wife, and
raising his mistress to the throne. Encouraged by the
nobles, the Archbishop proclaimed Catharine Empress of Russia, while Peter was lying drunk at his
chateau twenty-four miles from St. Petersburg, This
bold undertaking met with the hearty approval of the
people and the army. Her reign was a long one and
did much to raise Russia to its high position among
the nations. She died Nov. 10, 1796.

"Few sovereigns," says Allison, "will occupy a
more conspicuous place in the page of history, or
have left in their conduct on the throne, a more exalted reputation. Prudent in council, and intrepid in
conduct, cautious in forming resolutions, but vigorous in carrying them into execution; ambitious, but of
great and splendid objects only; passionately fond of
glory, without the alloy, at least in public affairs, of
sordid or vulgar inclinations; discerning in the choice
of her counsellors, and swayed in matters of state
only by lofty intellects; munificent in public, liberal in
private, firm in resolution, she dignified a despot's
throne by the magnanimity and patriotism of a more
virtuous age."[28]

"Victoria, Queen of England, and Empress of India, furnishes a still better illustration of the capacity
of woman to govern. For, she has not only proved
herself one of the first rulers of the age; but she has
given the world an illustrious example of noble womanhood in the several relations of daughter, wife and
mother.

"When a modest, shrinking girl of eighteen, she
was awakened early one morning, long before day,
by a visit from the Archbishop of Canterbury and
several nobles, who came to salute her as Queen of
England. She dropped upon her knees and begged
the archbishop to pray for her.

On the 20th of June, 1837, as she stood in an assembly composed of the highest nobility, veteran officers and statesmen of the Kingdom, she heard it officially proclaimed that "The high and mighty Princess, Alexandrina Victoria is the only lawful and rightful liege lady, and, by the grace of God, Queen of the United Kingdom of Great Britain and Ireland. Defender of the Faith." Overcome with emotion, she threw her arms around her mother's neck and burst into tears. The august assemblage was deeply moved. The young Queen soon won the hearts of her people.

No country of the world has been better governed than Great Britain has, during her long and peaceful reign. She has manifested the deepest interest in the highest welfare of her people, has selected wise and just, and patriotic men to administer the affairs of the government, and has pursued an equitable policy towards other nations. In the general upheaval among the thrones of Europe some years ago, hers remained secure, protected by the loving loyalty of her people. In her high position, her domestic example has been a great blessing to the world at large, while her beneficent reign has secured for her people unparalleled prosperity.

"We know," says Mill, "how small a number of reigning queens history presents, in comparison with that of Kings. Of this smaller number, a far larger proportion have shown talents for rule; though many of them have occupied the throne in difficult periods. It is remarkable, too, that they have, in a great number of instances, been distinguished by merits the most opposite to the imaginary and conventional character of women; they have been as much remarked for the firmness and vigor of their rule, as for its intelligence. When, to queens and empresses, we add regents, and viceroys of provinces, the list of women who have been eminent rulers of mankind swells to a great length."

"But," it is retorted, "women reign so successfully

by placing in important offices men of eminent ability."

The objection only proves the fitness of women to govern. The highest quality of a talent to rule, is the ability to select the most competent persons to fill the various subordinate offices. Napoleon not only knew how to plan a campaign, but he knew whom to select for officers to fight the battles. If woman possesses an instinctive insight into character, in a greater degree than man, then she is naturally, to that degree, in that respect, better fitted to fill positions of responsibility.

If she can, as she has done, successfully fill the thrones of Russia and Austria and Great Britain, then may she, with safety, be left free to fill any position in the church to which she may be called.

The church has no right to forbid the free exercise of abilities to do good which God has given. To do so is ursurpation and tyranny.

Men had better busy themselves in building up the temple of God, instead of employing their time in pushing from the scaffold their sisters, who are both able and willing to work with them side by side.

All restrictions to positions in the church based on race have been abolished; it is time then that those based on sex were also abolished.

CHAPTER XVI.

HEATHEN TESTIMONY.

"O, small shall seem all sacrifice
  And pain and loss,
When God shall wipe the weeping eyes,
For suffering give the victor's prize,
  The crown for cross!"

– Whittier.

PLINY, the younger, was born in Italy in A. D. 62. He was praetor under the Emperor Domitian, and Consul under Trajan. He was sent by the latter into Pontus and Bithynia as governor.

About the year 167, Pliny wrote the following letter to the Emperor Trajan. We give the translation of Dr. Nathaniel Lardner:

"Pliny to the Emperor Trajan wisheth health and happiness.

"It is my constant custom, sir, to refer myself to you in all matters concerning which I have any doubt, for who can better direct me where I hesitate, or instruct me where I am ignorant? I have never been present at any trials of Christians; so that I know not well what is the subject-matter of punishment, or of inquiry, or what strictness ought to be used in either. Nor have I been a little perplexed to determine whether any difference ought to be made upon account of age, or whether the young and tender, and the full-grown and robust, ought to be treated all alike: whether repentance should entitle to pardon, or whether all who have once been Christians ought to be punished, though they are now no longer so; whether the name itself although no crimes be detected, or crimes only belonging to the name ought to be punished. Concerning all these things I am in doubt.

"In the meantime I have taken this course with all who have been brought before me, and have been accused as Christians. I have put the question to them, whether they were Christians. Upon their confessing to me that they were, I repeated the question a second and a third time, threatening also to punish them with death. Such as still persisted, I ordered away to be punished; for it was no doubt with me, whatever might be the nature of their opinion, that contumacy, and inflexible obstinacy, ought to be punished. There were others of the same infatuation, whom, because they are Roman citizens, I have noted down to be sent to the city.

"In a short time, the crime spreading itself, even whilst under persecution, as is usual in such cases, divers sorts of people came in my way. An information was presented to me without mentioning the author, containing the names of many persons, who upon examination denied that they were Christians, or had ever been so; who repeated after me an invocation of the gods, and with wine and frankincense made supplication to your image, which for that purpose I have caused to be brought and set before them, together with the statues of the deities. Moreover, they reviled the name of Christ. None of which things, as is said, they who are really Christians can by any means be compelled to do. These, therefore, I thought proper to discharge.

"Others were named by an informer, who at first confessed themselves Christians, and afterwards denied it. The rest said they had been Christians, but had left them; some three years ago, and some longer, and one, or more, above twenty years. They all worshiped your image, and the statues of the gods; these also reviled Christ. They affirmed that the whole of their fault, or error, lay in this, that they were wont to meet together on a stated day before it was light, and sing among themselves alternately, a hymn to Christ, as a God, and bind themselves by an oath, not to the commission of any wickedness but not to be guilty of theft, or robbery, or adultery, never to falsify their word, nor to deny a pledge committed to them, when called upon to return it. When these things were performed, it was their custom to separate, and then to come together again to a meal, which they ate in common, without any disorder; but this they had forborne, since the publication of my edict, by which, according to your commands, I prohibited assemblies.

"After receiving this account I judged it the more necessary to examine, and that by torture, two maidservants, which were called ministers. But I have discovered nothing, beside a bad and excessive superstition.

"Suspending, therefore, all judicial proceedings, I have recourse to you for advice; for it has appeared unto me a matter highly deserving consideration, especially upon account of the great number of persons who are in danger of suffering. For many of all ages, and every rank, of both sexes likewise, are accused, and will be accused. Nor has the contagion of this superstition seized cities only, but the lesser towns, also, and the open country. Nevertheless, it seems to me that it may be restrained and corrected. It is certain that the temples, which were almost forsaken, begin to be more frequented. And the sacred solemnities, after a long intermission, are revived. Victims likewise are everywhere bought up, whereas for some time there were few purchasers. Whence it is easy to imagine what numbers of men might be reclaimed, if pardon were granted to those who shall repent."

So writes Pliny. We are now to observe the Emperor's rescript.

"Trajan to Pliny wisheth health and happiness.

"You have taken the right method, my Pliny, in your proceedings with those who have been brought before you as Christians; for it is impossible to establish any one rule that shall hold universally. They are not to be sought for. If any are brought before you, and are convicted, they ought to be punished. However, he that denies his being a Christian, and makes it evident in fact, that is, by supplicating to our gods, though he be suspected to have been so formerly, let him be pardoned upon repentance. But in no case of any crime whatever, may a bill of information be received without being signed by him who presents it; for that would be a dangerous precedent, and unworthy of my government."

There are many things in this letter of Pliny of great importance.

1. It shows the great influence that Christianity was already exerting upon the minds of the people. The temples of the gods *were almost forsaken.* Christianity spread so rapidly that it was called *a contagion.* It affected alike cities and towns and the open country.

2. It is a striking testimony to the purity of the character of these Christians. Though their enemies, to justify their treatment of them, accused them of gross crimes, a strict investigation resulted in finding that their lives were blameless and their adherence to the doctrines and morals of the Gospel firm and unwavering. They bound themselves by an oath, *not to the commission of any wickedness, but not to be guilty of theft, or robbery, or adultery, never to falsify their word, nor to deny a pledge committed to them, when called upon to return it.*

3. It shows that they held to the doctrine of the Divinity of Christ. They sang hymns *to Christ* as a God.

4. But the point to which I wish to call particular attention is the fact that the *Ministers of this church* were women. This is seen – 1. In Pliny's express statement, "which were called ministers." That women are meant is perfectly clear in the Latin word, ministrae, which is in the feminine gender. That this word is not used to designate their condition is plain; for that is expressed by the word *ancillis* – maid ser-

vants. 2. He would *naturally* examine the officers of the church.

Here is a governor possessed of arbitrary power. A hated, despised society is charged with secretly holding pernicious doctrines, and practicing abominable rites.

The governor is determined to go to the root of the matter, and ascertain the truth in the case. He examines witnesses in the usual way, and finds out nothing to their disadvantage. He now determines to adopt the last resort known to ancient despots, and to examine by torture. But who shall he examine? Who would he naturally select as being in possession of all the secrets of the society?

Evidently those who occupy the *highest position* in the society, who understand all its mysteries, and are acquainted with all its doings – its officers or teachers. So, too, when Pliny says that these two women *were called ministers,* he uses the term minister in the sense in which the Christians understood it – in the ecclesiastical sense. He does not himself call them "ministers;" if he did, it might be claimed that he uses the word in its secular sense, "a female attendant or assistant," though in the classics it is sometimes used to denote a "ministress at religious worship." But Pliny says, "they are called ministers," that is, by the Christians.

Nothing is said in this letter about bishops, or elders or deacons, or any other church officers.

It is not to be supposed that a man of Pliny's ability and learning, and discrimination would give his Emperor a carefully prepared description of a Christian church and make no mention of its officers or teachers. And he certainly does not unless these women were officers or teachers, or, as they *were called, ministers.*

Women, it seems, could be ministers of the church at this early age, while it was poor and persecuted, but after-wards, when it became rich and popular, they were set aside.

CHAPTER XVII.

CONCLUSION.

"What are we, what our race,
How good for nothing and base,
Without fair woman to aid us?
What could we do, where should we go,
How should we wander in night and wo,
    But for woman to lead us!"
                    *–CristovalDeCastillejo,*A.D.1590.

IN the preceding pages the following proposi-
tions have been clearly proved.

1. Man and woman were created equal, each possessing the same rights and privileges as the other.

2. At the fall, woman, because she was first in the
transgression, was, as a punishment, made subject to
her husband.

3. Christ re-enacted the primitive law and restored the original relation of equality of the sexes.

4. The objections to the equality of man and
woman in the Christian Church, based upon the
Bible, rest upon a wrong translation of some passages
and a misinterpretation of others.

The objections drawn from woman's nature are
fully overthrown by undisputed facts.

5. In the New Testament church, woman, as well
as man, filled the office of Apostle, Prophet, Deacon
or preacher, and Pastor. There is not the slightest evidence that the functions of any of these offices, when
filled by a woman, were different from what they
were when filled by a man.

6. Woman took a part in governing the Apostolic
church.

We come, then, to this final CONCLUSION: THE GOSPEL OF JESUS CHRIST, IN THE PROVISIONS WHICH IT MAKES, AND IN THE AGENCIES WHICH IT EMPLOYS, FOR THE SALVATION OF MANKIND, KNOWS NO DISTINCTION OF RACE, CONDITION, OR SEX, THEREFORE NO PERSON EVIDENTLY CALLED OF GOD TO THE GOSPEL MINISTRY, AND DULY QUALIFIED FOR IT, SHOULD BE REFUSED ORDI-NATION ON ACCOUNT OF RACE, CONDITION, OR SEX.

INDEX OF TEXTS.

FOOTNOTES

[1] T. Crawford in N.Y. Tribune, Feb. 22, 1891

[2] Book 1, Ch. 2, p. 4

[3] Book 2, Ch. 5, p. 13.

[4] Ch. 8, pp. 19, 20.

[5] Gibbon's Rome 4, 345.

[6] In Darkest Africa, vol. 2, p. 394.

[7] Woman, by L.P. Brackett, M.D., p. 55.

[8] Of Human Understanding, p. 335.

[9] Apology, p. 380.

[10] Apology, p. 413.

[11] P. 283

[12] Catechism p. 295.

[13] Presbyterian Review for 1886, June No.

[14] McClintock & Strong's Cyclopedia, Art. Ordination

[15] Killen, Ancient Church, p. 71, seq.

[16] Rev. W. Gould.

[17] See page 50.

[18] Subjection of Women, p. 48.

[19] Herodotus' History, IV:117.

[20] Herodotus' History, IX:27.

[21] Through the Dark Continent, V. 1, p. 400.

[22] V. 2, p. 330.

[23] Commentaries, v. 1, p. 176.

[24] Commentaries, v. 1, p. 176.

[25] Works, v. ix. p. 437.

[26] The Wesley Family, p. 412.

[27] History 4, 342, 3.

[28] History of Europe, Vol. 1, p. 425.

Printed in the United States
132797LV00002B/4/A

9 780893 671761